T0334592

DECISION-MAKING MANAGEMENT

DECISION-MAKING MANAGEMENT
A TUTORIAL AND APPLICATIONS

ALBERTO PLIEGO MARUGÁN

FAUSTO PEDRO GARCÍA MÁRQUEZ

ACADEMIC PRESS

An imprint of Elsevier

Academic Press is an imprint of Elsevier
125 London Wall, London EC2Y 5AS, United Kingdom
525 B Street, Suite 1800, San Diego, CA 92101-4495, United States
50 Hampshire Street, 5th Floor, Cambridge, MA 02139, United States
The Boulevard, Langford Lane, Kidlington, Oxford OX5 1GB, United Kingdom

Notices
Knowledge and best practice in this field are constantly changing. As new research and
experience broaden our understanding, changes in research methods, professional practices,
or medical treatment may become necessary.

Practitioners and researchers must always rely on their own experience and knowledge in
evaluating and using any information, methods, compounds, or experiments described
herein. In using such information or methods they should be mindful of their own safety and
the safety of others, including parties for whom they have a professional responsibility.

To the fullest extent of the law, neither the Publisher nor the authors, contributors, or editors,
assume any liability for any injury and/or damage to persons or property as a matter of
products liability, negligence or otherwise, or from any use or operation of any methods,
products, instructions, or ideas contained in the material herein.

Library of Congress Cataloging-in-Publication Data
A catalog record for this book is available from the Library of Congress

British Library Cataloguing-in-Publication Data
A catalogue record for this book is available from the British Library

ISBN 978-0-12-811540-4

For information on all Academic Press publications
visit our website at https://www.elsevier.com/books-and-journals

Working together
to grow libraries in
developing countries

www.elsevier.com • www.bookaid.org

Publisher: Nikki Levy
Acquisition Editor: Graham Nisbet
Editorial Project Manager: Susan Ikeda
Production Project Manager: Poulouse Joseph
Cover Designer: Mark Rogers

Typeset by SPi Global, India

CONTENTS

LIST OF FIGURES

LIST OF TABLES

AUTHORS

Alberto Pliego Marugán received his International Doctorate at the School of Industrial Engineers of Ciudad Real in 2016. In 2013, he completed MSc in Industrial Engineering from by the University of Castilla-La Mancha (UCLM), Ciudad Real, Spain. From 2012, he is engineer by UCLM (Ciudad Real) and, from 2009, he is technical engineer by UCLM (Ciudad Real).

He has given some lectures on occupational risk prevention and organization of the production in the E.I.M.I.A. (Almadén, Spain). He has also taken classes in signal processing and industrial management at the UCLM.

Between 2012 and 2013, he worked as solution assistant in Everis Spain S.L. His principal roles in this project were the resolution of incidents, unitary testing, and programming in COBOL, Host, and JCL.

From Jun. 2013 to present, he is a member of Ingenium Research Group and he is collaborating in national and international research projects with the Business Management Department of the University of Castilla-La Mancha. He also has contributed as author in several journal papers, books, conferences, and book chapters.

Fausto Pedro García Márquez obtained his European Doctorate in 2004 at the University of Castilla-La Mancha (UCLM, Spain) with a maximum distinction. He has been a distingue with the Best paper awarded in Renewable Energy (3.5 JCR, 2015), Runner Prize (2015), Advancement Prize (2013), and Silver Prize (2012) by the International Society of Management Science and Engineering Management, or the Advancement Prize in the Third International Conference on Management Science and Engineering Management, etc. He is working at UCLM as Full Professor accredited, Spain, Honorary Senior Research Fellow at Birmingham University, United Kingdom, Lecturer at the Postgraduate European Institute, and he was Senior Manager in Accenture (2013–14).

Fausto has managed a great number of projects: 5 European projects as Principal Investigator (PI), 4 FP7 framework programs and 1 Euroliga, being researcher in 3 FP7; PI in 4 national projects, and 2 as researcher; 4 Regional Projects, 1 as PI and 3 as researcher; 3 University Projects, 1 as PI and 2 as researcher; and more than 100 with research institutes and industrial companies (98% as director). He has been evaluator in different programs, both national and international.

As a result of the research work, he has published more than 150 papers (65% in ISI journals, 30% in JCR journals, and 92% internationals), being the main author of 68 publications. Some of these papers have been especially recognized, e.g., by "Renewable Energy" (as "Best Paper Award 2014"); "International Society of Management Science and Engineering Management" (as "excellent"); and by the "International Journal of Automation and Computing" and "IMechE Part F: Journal of Rail and Rapid Transit" (most downloaded), etc. He is the author and editor of 18 books (Elsevier, Springer, Pearson, Mc-GrawHill, Intech, IGI, Marcombo, AlfaOmega, etc.), and he is holder of five patents.

He is Director of Ingenium Research Group. It is an international and multidisciplinary research group, with nine members from University of

Castilla-La Mancha (UCLM) and CUNEF, and thirteen members of national and internationals institutions. He is also Editor-in-Chief of International Journal of Engineering and Technologies, and Associate Editor of the international journals: Engineering Management Research, Open Journal of Safety Science and Technology, and has participated as Committee Member in more than 25 International Conferences.

FOREWORD

DM processes are critical predictors and contributors for success. The intense competition among companies requires rapid strategic responses and actions. Companies are exposed to a vast amount of input due to the volume of information available in the information age, but the input data must be processed and converted into useful information to be of real value. The complexity of data processing is exponential in light of the amount of data.

This book addresses essential issues for both practitioners and academicians. The book contains pedagogical examples that assist in understanding the DM process. There are several appendices that contain detailed case studies with examples, illustrations, and lessons learned. The methods employed require basic knowledge of statistics and a familiarity of the system that will be analyzed.

The book introduces the different stages of DM throughout history. It takes us through several important historical milestones, from the first philosophers who contemplated Decision Sciences to the current Decision Support Systems. DM knowledge was required in the construction of the Pyramids, building of early sea vessels, and during the industrial revolution. DM has always been part of human development throughout history and will undoubtedly remain so in perpetuity.

The authors demonstrate that the appropriate use of information increases the probability of good solutions. The reader observes some methods of organizing available information with simple rules that can synthesize information automatically. The key strength of these techniques is the ability to efficiently consider a wide range of variables. These variables can represent various factors, which contribute to the decision process. The variables can be exogenous or endogenous and can represent requirements, preferences, constraints, etc. In addition, the decisions may be affected by nonquantitative factors, e.g., political, social, ethical, or legal. The flexibility of the methods proposed in the book allows for formulating and solving almost any problem.

The book proposes solving a main problem by considering all possible subproblems. Models are used to measure how important a specific variable is within the main problem. These models are called "importance measures." The importance measures are calculated by solving the main problem and the subproblems. The impact of each variable on the global system can be crucial information if an investment for the system is needed. The methods proposed allow for optimizing fiscal considerations and resource allocation; reducing manpower needs; and, increasing productivity.

DM processes exist for immediate decisions, periodic decisions, or long-term decisions. The methods proposed in the book can also use time-dependent models to facilitate future decisions. This capability can be useful for future scenarios, and therefore, can be used to determine possible future threats, strengths, and/or weaknesses. This will provide competitive advantages to companies that can effectively adapt strategies.

DM is a process in which the best decisions are made when using information properly and efficiently and when a wide range of possibilities and actions are considered.

In summary, the main focus of the book is to offer insight into methodologies for DM in cases that involve an abundance of information.

Benjamin Lev
Drexel University, Philadelphia, PA, United States

PREFACE

The manner in which decision making (DM) has been carried out throughout history has been influenced by the social, historical, and technological context, but in every case it has had the common objective of providing solutions according to the decision maker.

This book presents an exhaustive study on the DM process and provides some methodologies to address the problems that can arise in the course of professional and academic activities. The main objective of the book is to describe techniques for smart and optimal use of the available information to make the decision successful.

Chapter 1 introduces the main concept of the term "DM," and it is contextualized from its beginnings to the present. Different types of decisions are explained and classified. The importance of the management and control activities for the current business is highlighted. Finally, a brief introduction to Logical Decision Trees (LDT) is shown as a preface of Chapter 2.

Chapter 2 defines LDT as an essential method to solve the paradigm proposed in this book. A complete definition and description of this method is given in this chapter. Moreover, different analyses that can be carried out, such as importance analysis, sensitivity study, etc., are shown in this section.

BDD are introduced in Chapter 3, will be employed together with logical trees (LT). These diagrams contribute to optimizing the computational analysis of the LDT and, therefore, to improve the efficiency of the approach. Several techniques to carry out the conversion from LT to BDD are employed and analyzed together.

Chapter 4 is a didactical and practical chapter in which some examples of conversion are presented, solved and explained. Different characteristics are considered to take into account a large range of possibilities for converting LDT into BDD. Moreover, an estimation of the computational cost of the LDT direct resolution is described. A list of advantages of the use of BDD is also shown.

Chapter 5 describes the main advantages of using the approaches proposed in this book, the dynamic analysis. This chapter will present the case studies in which the problem is addressed over the time. These examples reveal that it is possible to make the best decision.

Chapter 6 proposes two novel methods for optimizing the DM processes. The first method, a mathematical optimization approach, uses the expression provided by a BDD as an object function for a programming problem. This is a novel use of a Boolean function. The second method is an adaptation of an importance measure to consider possible exogenous decision variables, e.g., costs. Both methods are limited by the possibility of building a LDT that represents the problem with a correct accuracy.

Finally, several annexes provide useful information of the methods and the theory explained in the book.

This book is intended for anyone who is responsible for making decisions in any firm. It can also be a very useful text for those students or general public who want to practice and learn the importance of DM processes.

Alberto Pliego Marugán
Fausto Pedro García Márquez

NOMENCLATURE

BDD	binary decision diagrams
BFS	breath first search
CCO	common cause occurrences
CS	cut-set
CCF	common cause failure
DAG	direct acyclic graph
DFS	depth first search
DIF	diagnostic importance factor
DM	DM
DSS	decision support system
IM	importance measure
ITE	If-Then-Else
KKT	Karush-Khun-Tucker
LDT	logical decision tree
LDTA	logical decision tree analysis
MCS	minimal cut-set
MI	maximum investment
MIF	marginal importance factor
MOB	multiple occurring branches
MOE	multiple occurring event
MP	main problem
NDF	normal dilemma form
NLPP	nonlinear programming problem
OBDD	ordered binary decision diagram
PI	prime implicants
ROBDD	reduced ordered binary decision diagram
RAW	risk achievement worth
RRW	risk reduction worth
SDP	sum of disjoint products
TDLR	top-down left-right

SUMMARY

Decision making is defined and contextualized from its beginnings to contemporary days. Different types of decisions are described and classified for any business. The importance of the management and control activities for the current business is highlighted. Logical decision trees (LDT) are described in detail. LDT are employed in the methodologies proposed in this book. A detailed definition and explanation of this tool is done. A set of stages are established to carry out a qualitative and a quantitative analysis of a system. Different types of analysis, such as importance analysis, sensitivity analysis, etc. are presented. The main measures and methods such as Fussel-Vesely, Birnbaum, Criticality, AND method, etc. are presented. BDD are obtained from LDT. The theoretical basis of this conversion is widely explained with several examples. The result of this conversion is influenced by the variable ranking. The main ranking methods are introduced and a comparison between them is shown. It is also considered how to perform a quantitative analysis using the expression of the occurrence probability of the top event. Different characteristics are considered to take into account a wide range of possibilities for converting LDTs to BDDs. A comparative study shows the advantages and drawbacks of both tools. A new approach is developed to estimate the computational cost of solving a certain system through its corresponding LDT. A dynamic analysis is presented to consider the behavior of the system over time. The probability assignation is done by time dependent models. Reliable forecasts are made by these analyses. Two novel methods for optimizing the decision-making process are explained. The first method, a mathematical optimization approach, uses the Boolean function provided by a BDD as the object function for a programming problem. A mathematical background on nonlinear programming problems is provided to facilitate the comprehension of this method. The second approach is an adaptation of the Birnbaum importance measure to consider possible exogenous decision variables, e.g., costs. A case study is solved by employing both methods, being the results analyzed and compared. The methods are limited by the possibility of building a LDT that represents the problem with a good accuracy.

CHAPTER 1

Introduction

1.1 BACKGROUND

Aristocracies were originally the main model of governance almost throughout our history. During this time, the important decisions were made by the ruling family. The problem of making decisions by an appropriate use of the intellect, art, scientific knowledge, wisdom, prudence, and understanding, was addressed in the fourth century B.C by *Aristotle*.[1] There are some modern studies asserting the idea that *Jesus Christ* was a paradigmatic decision maker.[2] Thereby, some biblical events, such as the selection of the twelve disciples or the establishment of a hierarchy by Moses, have been considered as managerial choices.[3]

Industrial revolution, as some political revolutions in America and France, caused a shift from aristocracy to bureaucracy. Most relevant decisions were made by people with power whereas uneducated workers were complying with orders and with a great effort to use rationality in *DM (DM)* processes, but without any technical knowledge about DM. *Daniel Bernoulli* in 1738 introduced the "*Decision Theory.*" In the situations treated by *decision theorist*, choices are made in a nonrandom way. Two centuries later, *Frank Ramsey* conducted further studies about decision theory through subjective probability.[3] *Condorcet*, in 1793, developed the theory of voting on collective DM based on the following principle: an alternative that defeats every other by a simple majority is the socially optimal choice.[4]

Almost half a century later, *Charles Babbage*, considered as the father of computation, developed a complex machine called the analytical engine. It will set the transition from mechanized arithmetic to the computational based on information systems, being the basis of modern decision support systems.[5] In 1911, *Frederick Taylor*, one of the "fathers of the management science"[6] delivered the idea that there is "one way best" to do a job.[7]

By the middle of 20th century, several approaches on "*classic decision theory*" were carried out, being one of the most important the "*bounded rationality,*" by Simon.[8] It is based on the idea that the available information, cognitive limitation of the mind, and the time finite, limit the rationality of individuals to DM. Some important researchers in this field were: *Barnard*

Decision-Making Management
http://dx.doi.org/10.1016/B978-0-12-811540-4.00001-6

imported the term DM from administrative activities to managerial and economic activities[9]; *Wald* published *"Statistical Decision Functions,"* based on decision models that were built by ranking alternatives depending on their worst outcomes[10]; *Zadeh* introduced a new approach about how to treat with uncertainty[11]; *Savage* provides a statistical model for decision and a coherent framework for DM[12]; *Neumann and Morgenstern* established the essential axioms to build a utility function,[13] conceived a ground-breaking mathematical theory of games of strategy. Theory of games not only would revolutionize economics, but also form the entirely new field of science named *"game theory,"* used to analyze real-word phenomena.

In 1960, *Warren Bennis* predicted the bureaucracies were dying due to obsolete procedures on DM.[3] Stable industrial environments paved the way to greater employee involvement in organizational DM processes. This and the inexorable sophistication of information systems referenced the way to a new era on DM processes. *James Clawson* identified it as a change from bureaucracies to a form of organization in which the basis of power is information. This new form of organization was named *"infocracy."*[14] *Decision Support System* (DSS) began to appear in the 1960s as a result of the technology progress, together with the necessity of devices to help managers in DM processes.[5] DSS was used to examine investment plans and then, it has been used for fixing prices, publicity, logistic, etc. until today.

1.2 INTRODUCTION TO THE DECISION MAKING

DM is a selection method. It is daily used in a personal and professional context. There are a large number of times where DM is carried out. Decisions can require weeks, even months in order to reach the correct alternative.

In a DM scenario, it is commonly known that there is an event that is (not) desired, which entail a path among the different alternatives that let to reach the objective.[15] In any case, the optimal situation is desired, i.e., the one which will provide the best results.[16] With this purpose, it is essential to select different criteria that allow for discerning the scenarios to choose the best.[17]

DM can be defined also as: "the research of identifying and choosing alternatives based on the decision-maker's weighs/values and preferences. All be possible alternatives must be identified for making a decision. Then the best alternative is chosen regarding to the goals, constraints, etc."[18]

Forrester defines the DM as the transformation process from data to proceedings.[19] The data collection is a strategy for DM, and consequential proceedings are possible to be carried out. Feedback is obtained with the proceedings, which helps to keep improving the problem and giving more data to the system. It suggests that DM requires a continuous communication process, where the data obtained leads to an improvement of the available information.

DM must be carried out when a certain problem occurs. It would be desired to be able to discern whether there is a real problem in a business. Ref. 20 proposed to solve if a mismatch is found by focusing on finding the difference between the real and the ideal, or desired, scenario. The main role of the DM is to reduce the difference.[21]

Decision may be defined as: "a thorough selection of proceedings among available alternatives, aiming a desired result, knowing the resources are limited."[22]

There are several alternatives to classify the decisions made in a business.[23] According to the needs developed in this book, they are classified as shown in Fig. 1.1.

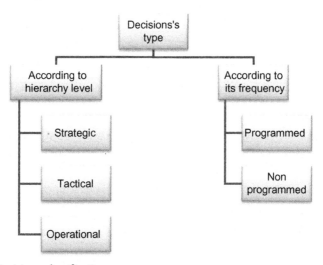

Fig. 1.1 Decisions classification.

Strategic decisions are those defined on the lines of the objectives and proceedings to be followed by the business. There is a shortage in data, and its impact on the business is crucial. Wrong strategic decisions may lead to the business's bankruptcy. A high degree of knowledge is required. Managers are responsible for this kind of decisions.

Tactical decisions occur with major incidence than the strategic decisions. Procedures and routines are developed to control them. Enough data about how to analyze them is commonly available. Wrong tactical decisions may bring troubles to the business, but a solution could be given without the business's bankruptcy. Lower level managers are usually responsible for these decisions.

Finally, the *operational decisions* is to carry out strategic decisions. Junior managers and general workers are generally responsible for them. Wrong operational decisions have no far-reaching implications for the future and may be fixed easily.

Programmed decisions are repeated frequently in a business according to its frequency. A procedure is carried out every time it occurs.

On the other hand, *nonprogrammed decisions are* those that emerge unexpectedly. Decision makers need to take decisions employing their awareness and experience. Usually it involves a high degree of difficulty, and must be done by experts in the field.

The DM process described in this book is focused on a *Main Problem* (*MP*), which represents an undesired (desired) event whose occurrence probability needs to be minimized (maximized). The logical structure of the MP is approached by a LDT. The following main scenarios can be distinguished according to the information available in the DM process[24]:

- *DM under certainty*: The problem is entirely known and every feasible state for all the variables are known, and any consequences of each decision can be completely achieved.
- *DM under risk*: It implies partial information, and some information to the problem is stochastic. This will be the scenario considered in this book.
- *DM under uncertainty*: Information about the MP and its causes is not complete, and part of the information is missing.[24]

1.3 OVERVIEW OF APPROACHES FOR DECISION MAKING

There are many studies that present different models for DM, e.g., cost-benefit analysis; elementary methods,[25] such as *pros* and *cons* analysis; "maximin" and "maximax" methods; conjunctive and disjunctive methods; lexicographic method; simple multiattribute rating technique; generalized means; the analytic hierarchy process; outranking methods; ELECTRE and PROMETHEE[25]; the fuzzy preference relations[26]; cognitive decision-making models[27]; large group DM methods[28,29]; etc. Moreover, there are a large amount of studies about DM processes under risk contexts. Some of the most important models are collected in references.[30–36] There are also some important research works focused on the industrial DM processes, for example, the multicriteria decision model.[37,38]

This book proposes a new way of solving DM problems through the linkage of graphical and mathematical tools. The first method, based on mathematical optimization approach, uses the expression provided by a BDD as an object function for a programming problem. This is a novel use of a Boolean function. Regarding the second method, called Birnbaum-cost measure method, the novelty lies in the adaptation of the Birnbaum measure to consider possible decision variables such as costs. Both methods are limited by the possibility of building a LDT that represents the problem with a correct accuracy.

It is important to remark that these methods can be applied to other decision problems,[23] e.g., employed in the design stage of products,[39] or to elaborate preventive or predictive maintenance plans.[40–42] In general, they could be used for addressing those problems where a logical function can be defined and several alternatives can be considered.

1.4 MANAGEMENT PLANNING AND CONTROL

Planning is "one of the chief administrative roles, which is circumscribed as the rational process of DM to select the right future course among different alternatives. Its fundamental goal is to narrow the gap between the current situation and the desired one."[43]

Planning is important because it shows the feasible solutions and make available a pathway. It will make it possible to take part in the DM and act in accordance with it. Planning seeks to solve the following questions:

- Which is the main objective and which is the process to achieve the mentioned objective?
- How is it possible to trace a start-up plan to achieve the objective?
- Which departments will be involved and what resources will be needed?
- Is it worth the money/resources and time invested over this problem?
- What will be the impact on the business?

A precise planning without a subsequent *control* may lead to a mismatch in the business objectives, because it will not be totally clear whether the planning is performed right or wrong. Therefore, even though the best planning is carried out, if it is not managed by the control, it will become completely ineffective.

Business control can be classified depending on the course of action[44]:

- Previous control
- Constant/current control
- Subsequent control

In previous control, preventing the problem is desired. A start-up and revision procedure is needed to carry out the planning required to perform mentioned prevention. Current control verifies whether the planning is being achieved in the same manner as it had been formerly established. Finally, subsequent control evaluates the obtained results and crosschecks whether they are as expected.

Control process is closely linked to the existence of the following variables[45]:

- An indicator that allows orientating and evaluating each department performance.
- A predictive model that makes it possible to provide prior estimate of the result of an action, which will be carried out by the managers.
- A business strategy.
- Some department information about the performance and result of its operation.
- The appraisal of each DM made by any department in the business.

Furthermore, a procedure must be carried out to get the results as close as possible to reality. The procedure considers:

- To gather as much data as possible.
- To compare and contrast the data against the established goals.
- Finally, whenever a mismatch is found, execute corrective measures.

Management control is defined as a complete set of techniques used to regulate properly such that the planning is being achieved precisely. "*Management control's main purpose is to handle and monitor the goals, plans, management programs and decisions, needing continuous information obtained through the specific areas and techniques.*"[44]

Management control system is considered a system whereby data and control are closely linked to the resource management and business. The main purpose is to ensure that the objectives have been successfully completed and to propose corrective measures whenever it is needed.

Moreover, management control must be understood as a dynamic control, i.e., a system capable to change on time and to respond to continuous changes. A business having a precise management will be more efficient and effective, and it will be also able to deal with the ongoing problems as they appear.

Control systems, particularly those that are intended to analyze companies' situations similar to the ones above explained, must be processed as dynamic systems, i.e., exogenous influences must be taken into account when its influence becomes more important.

Management control will turn into the most important approach. It helps in the quantitative analysis in DM and it is also in charge of controlling the whole process. It leads to understanding of the results, and provides a framework which encompasses this type of business issues.

1.5 LOGICAL DECISION TREES

The *structure function* is a logical function that defines the condition of the system. This condition is provided by the condition of the events[1] that compose the system $x = (x_1, x_2, ..., x_n)$, where x_i are logical variables that represent the condition of each event. In this study, the structure function is considered as a binary function, i.e., the events that can only get one of the two possible states: occurrence and nonoccurrence.

A *LDT* is a graphical representation of a structure function. A LDT structure consists of a root node (*top event*) that is broken down into various nodes located below, where the nodes can be events, logical gates, and branches. A specific set of symbols is used to represent each type of node (see Annex B), called LDT system of symbols.

The basic events are logical variables that adopt two possible states: 1 if the basic event occurs, and 0 if it does not occur. The gates are logical operators that connect the events. They establish the Boolean expression of the system when the LDT is read from the basic events to the top event. The *Boolean algebra* (see Annex A) is the main approach to operate with these logical expressions, i.e., an algebraic structure that synthesizes the mentioned expressions. Fig. 1.2 shows the stages to be followed in the LDT analysis.

The following types of *events* can be identified in a LDT:
- *Top event*: This is the event placed at the highest level of the LDT. It represents the main cause, or the affair that is pretended to be studied.
- *Basic events*: They cannot be broken down into more elementary events.
- *Intermediate events*: They can be broken down into more elementary events and are located under a logical gate.

---

[1] The term "*event*" can represent a cause, a success, etc.

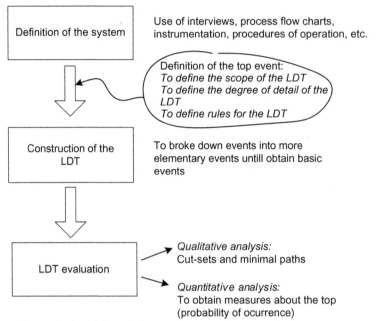

Fig. 1.2 Stages in the LDT analysis.

1.6 TYPES OF LOGICAL DECISION TREES

LDTs can be classified according to their size and complexity, the number of logical gates, etc. The following classification is done as a function of the number of events[46]:

- *Small LDTs* (number of events < 100)
- *Medium LDTs* (100 < number of events < 1000)
- *Large LDTs* (number of events > 1000)

The classification regarding to the logical gates is:

- *Static LDTs*: They are only formed by conventional logical gates: AND, OR, and VOTING OR (k-out-of-n).
- *Dynamic LDTs*: They are composed of conventional gates and other logical gates with dynamic nature as: Exclusive OR (XOR), Priority AND (PAND), Sequence Enforcing (SEQ), and SPARE gates.

A LDT is *coherent* when a certain event and its negation do not appear simultaneously. According to the coherence, the LDTs are classified as[46]:

- *Coherent LDTs*: A LDT is coherent when a certain event and its negation do not appear simultaneously, i.e., a coherent LDT cannot include any

NOT gate. The study presented is focused on coherent LDTs because otherwise the operations become very complex.

- *Non-Coherent LDTs*: They include NOT gates and, therefore, a certain event and its negation could appear simultaneously. In a noncoherent LDT, the top event can occur when a certain event has not occurred.

1.7 TERMINOLOGY OF COMPLEX LOGICAL DECISION TREES

A LDT could be formed by *multiple occurring events* (*MOEs*), i.e., these LDTs present redundancies. It is possible that a certain LDT appears more than once in the LDT, i.e., there are *multiple occurring branches* (*MOB*). All the events that belong to same MOB are MOE.

Very large and/or complex LDTs can be simplified into smaller and/or less complex LDTs. These LDTs are called modules. A module can only have one output to the rest of the LDTs, and it cannot have any input from the LDT. Two modules are considered *s-independents* when there is no any event that belongs to both of them. A module is considered to be dynamic if:

- The top gate of the module is dynamic.
- The top gate of the module is not dynamic but there are LDTs that are not *s-independents* in this module.

Chapters 3 and 4 present a method based on the conversion from LDTs to BDDs. This method allows obtaining an analytical expression of the occurrence probability of the top event regarding the probabilities of the basic events. This expression defines quantitatively the behavior of a whole system or process, but it does not take into account the exogenous variables that can be more influential than the endogenous ones.

A novel dynamic analysis approach is presented in Chapter 5, where are included different case studies. Chapter 6 describes a robust and flexible method to consider exogenous variables that may be important for optimizing the DM processes. This approach employs the analytical expression obtained from the BDD as the objective function of a nonlinear programming problem (NLPP) where the external factors are modeled by a set of constraints.

CHAPTER 2

Logical Decision Tree Analysis

2.1 INTRODUCTION

Logical decision tree analysis (LDTA) is a technique based on symbolic logic that is applied in the study of DM. It is a deductive method that considers a set of events with their root causes. The LDT is an organized graphical representation of an event set connected by logic gates. Any LDT has different combinations of basic events, whose simultaneous occurrence causes the occurrence of the top event.

2.2 STAGES OF THE ANALYSIS

LDTA process can be defined by different approaches according to the method employed. This book proposes a method based on a linear process for increasing the benefit of use of the variables considered and, therefore, the DM function. This analysis consists of the following steps[47]:

- To understand and design the problem, employing flow charts, drawings, instrumentation, operating procedures, etc.
- Definition of the top event.
- To develop the LDT.
- To collect the dataset, defining models to describe the behavior of each component, employing revisions, interviews, etc.
- Quantitative assessment of the LDT, where the numerical values of the variables are obtained under certain conditions.

Other references consider the analysis by emphasizing the interrelation between the different stages and feedbacks, for example Stamatelatos (2012) proposes the scheme given in Fig. 2.1.[48]

The four basic stages can be distinguished for a LDTA in detail in reference,[49] taking into account the system definition, construction of the LDT, qualitative analysis, and quantitative analysis.

2.2.1 System Definition

The system definition will be employed to set the objective of the analysis, which has a direct impact on the design and development of the LDT. The

Decision-Making Management
http://dx.doi.org/10.1016/B978-0-12-811540-4.00002-8

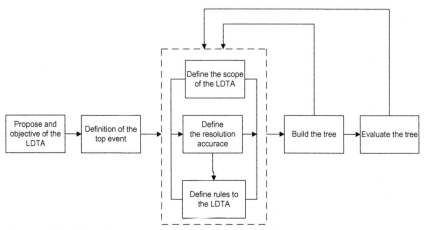

Fig. 2.1 Schedule in the LDT analysis.

information is collected, e.g., a description of all events. Each component will be disaggregated until the required degree of detail is reached. It can be done by:

- Flowcharts or block charts.
- Functional diagrams.
- Definitions of objectives and modes of operation.

The flowcharts and functional diagrams require the information about the events and the relationships between them. The boundary conditions of the system must be set, e.g., the degree of detail, internal and external conditions, etc. External conditions determine the scope of the analysis, and the degree of detail will provide the accuracy of the analysis.

2.2.2 Construction of Logical Decision Trees

The construction method depends on the objective, the scope, and the resolution. It can be done as:

1. Identification of the objective of the LDTA.
2. Definition of the top event.
3. Scope of the LDTA.
4. Definition of the degree of detail of the LDTA.
5. Defining rules for the LDTA.

The top event can represent, for example, a strategic decision, an investment, loss of landing gear, etc. The scope definition is used for choosing the events that will be included in the LDT. The scope includes design of the system, the time period, and the boundary conditions for the analysis (initial states of the events and the system inputs), i.e., the LDTA is done in a certain time and conditions.

The LDT structure, i.e., the number of the events, levels, and logical gates, will be detailed according to the accuracy of the results. The construction of the LDT is done from the top event to the events connected via logical gates. The events are broken down into more elementary events, etc., and finally into the basic events. The main construction methods can be classified based on the following criteria:

- The model of the system.
- The algorithm to obtain the LDT.
- The way that the knowledge is used.

The construction is an iterative process that can be divided as:

1. The *"father"* events (causes) must be identified for each event. They are necessary and sufficient events that cause the *"son"* event (effect).
2. To categorize each causal *event* as *primary* or *secondary*. If there are different categories of causal events, it is habitual to use the rule of including an OR gate in the events from left to right in the order listed.
3. To define the status of each event, e.g., the probability of the event.

The basic events at the same level under a logical gate must be independent between them. Other rules are:

- When there are more than two branches for a gate, it must be set converging into a single input branch to the gate.
- An event must be located between two gates to avoid the direct connection of two logical gates.

The construction of a LDT can be very complicated when a large and/or complex system is treated. However, there have been important advances to facilitate it. Although the software for the LDT construction is useful, it is necessary and unavoidable to make a final detailed review of the LDT by an expert.

2.2.3 Qualitative Evaluation

The *qualitative analysis* provides information about the interrelationships between the occurrences of basic events and the top event. The *structure function* is a logical function that can be expressed in different equivalent forms. For example, it is usually defined as any logic function that can be expressed in the first *canonical form*, also called *normal dilemma form* (*NDF*), or *sum of disjoint products* (*SDP*), that is a sum of products ("minterms") of logical variables. Each term represents a sufficient combination of basic events that causes the occurrence of the top event.

The information gathered from a qualitative analysis is:
- *Cut-sets* (*CS*).
- *Minimal paths*.

A CS is a combination of basic events whose simultaneous occurrence causes the occurrence of the top event. A *minimal CS* (*MCS*) is a "minimum" combination of basic events whose simultaneous occurrence causes the occurrence of the top event. A "minimum" combination is defined as a necessary and sufficient combination to cause the occurrence of the top event, i.e., a MCS would not be a CS if any of its basic events did not happen. For noncoherent structures, the MCSs are called *prime implicants* (PIs). In case of coherent systems, they are called MCSs.

A *minimal path* set is a "minimum" combination of events whose simultaneous operation (nonoccurrence of events) ensures the system operation (no occurrence of the top event), i.e., if any of the events of a minimal path set occurs, then the top event occurs.

The PIs (or MCSs) are unique and independent of the equivalent forms that a structure function can have. The structure function can be expressed as a sum of PIs (or MCSs):

$$\varphi(x_1, x_2, \ldots, x_n) = \sum_{j=1}^{m} P_j, \quad \text{where } P_j = \prod x_i \tag{2.1}$$

There are *direct methods* applied to the LDT, and *indirect methods* in which equivalent graphs are used to study the structure function, to determine the PIs (or MCSs) from the LDT. The methods employed are not based on previous identification of the CS. It is not possible to produce a complete list of all groups in large LDTs. It is usual to choose only the CSs that contribute most significantly to the occurrence of the top event to address this problem. The main direct methods are:
- *Simulation methods*: Random conditions are generated for the basic events. The structure function is evaluated for each condition vector.
- *Deterministic methods*: The structure function is transformed applying mathematical expressions to obtain a NDF form that consists on PIs or MCSs. The main algorithms to achieve this objective are: Mucus, factoring–division, addition & test logic, OR–EOR, truncation, and modularization.

The main indirect method is BDD. They are data structures that represent the structure function and work directly with logical expressions rather than with CSs. A detailed description of BDDs is presented in Chapter 3.

2.2.4 Quantitative Evaluation

The quantitative evaluation is normally used to obtain information about the top event. The main methodologies to carry out a quantitative analysis can be divided into three sections:

- *Methods based on the use of PIs*. A qualitative analysis is done to determine the CSs, and it is used to perform probabilistic approaches.
- *Direct evaluation methods*. A previous qualitative evaluation is not required because they work directly with the structure function.
- *Methods based on BDDs*. The LDT is converted to a BDD.

2.3 Importance Analysis

The *importance measures* (*IMs*) are used to quantify the influence of a certain event in the behavior of a system. They give an index that provides the influence of the event to the occurrence of the top event. IMs provide a quantitative index of the influence of each basic event on the occurrence of the top event. Generally, an event is more relevant to the occurrence of the top event when its IM is higher.

The main applications of the IMs are:

- *Design, research and development of a system, product, or process*: There are often limited resources to improve a system, i.e., it is essential to identify the most important events to allocate the resources in an optimal way. The IMs provide useful information to assign the resources because they show the events that generate the greatest probabilities of the top event when they are improved.
- *Conversion from LDTs to BDDs*: A ranking of events generated using the structural importance[1] will establish a proper ranking to obtain smaller BDDs.
- *Predictive and/or preventive tasks*: A list of importance is useful for prioritizing inspections and planning tasks.

---

[1] Structural IMs have a deterministic nature (nonprobabilistic).

The IMs can be divided into two categories from a probabilistic point of view:

- *Deterministic.* IM determines the importance of an event without taking into account its probability of occurrence. It is useful in the design stage where the information about the occurrence of the events is limited. These measures depend on the position of the event within the LDT structure.
- *Probabilistic.* IMs provide more information about the system than the deterministic IMs. In this case, the importance of each event depends on its occurrence probability and its position in the system.

It is desirable to get a list of events ranked from highest to lowest importance measures. There are different criteria to generate this ranking, called "events ranking."

The *ranking methods*, e.g., Fussell-Vesely and Birnbaum, are applied to the LDTs when they have been developed and all the probabilities of occurrence are known, i.e., these IMs cannot be applied in the design and development stages.

It is desirable that the ranking will be the same when different methods are applied, in other cases the best IM is not clear. In these cases, an average of the most important measures, e.g., Fussell, Birnbaum and Criticality, can be considered, and the obtained ranking will be a consensus between the three measures.

2.3.1 Fussell-Vesely

The *Fussell-Vesely* IM was introduced by J.Fussell and W.E. Vesely in the early 70s.[50] Sometimes, it is called *diagnostic importance factor* (DIF). This IM is constructed using MCSs. The probability of the union of all the MCSs is the probability of occurrence of the top event.

An IM associated with each basic event is the probability of the union of all the MCSs that contain the event, i.e., the probability that the top event occurs due to the occurrence of any CS that contains the event. This IM does not measure the probability of occurrence of the top event due to a basic event, however it is an indicator of the future importance of this event.

Fussell-Vesely IM is defined for coherent LDTs as the quotient between the probability of the union of the CSs that contain an event and the probability of the top event. The Fussell-Vesely IM, I^{FV}, is given by Eq. (2.2).

$$I_i^{FV} = \frac{P\left(e_1^i \cup e_2^i \cup e_2^i \ldots e_n^i\right)}{Q_{Sys}} \quad (2.2)$$

where $P\left(e_1^i \cup e_2^i \cup e_2^i \ldots e_n^i\right)$ is the probability of the union of all the CSs that contain the event i. Q_{Sys} is the probability of occurrence of the top event.

This variable will be noted as Q_{MP} (probability of the MP) in this book. Q_{sys} will be used for generic examples, and Q_{MP} will be employed for specific DM case studies. On the other hand, the events will be noted as "e_i" for generic cases, and the events of DM case studies will be noted as BC_i (Basic Causes).

The numerator is usually approximated by the sum of the probabilities of all the MCSs that contain the basic event i.

2.3.2 Birnbaum

The *Birnbaum* IM was introduced by Z.W. Birnbaum in 1969, during his research on the reliability of multicomponent systems.[51] The Birnbaum IM is also called *marginal importance factor*.

Birnbaum IM is defined as the probability that the system is in a critical condition with respect to a certain event, i.e., the system varies from a state of nonoccurrence to a state of occurrence due to the occurrence of the event. Birnbaum developed this measurement, I^{Birn}, for coherent LDTs, defined by Eq. (2.5).

$$I^{Birn} = \frac{\partial Q_{Sys}}{\partial q_i} \quad (2.3)$$

where $Q_{Sys} = Q(q_1, q_2, \ldots, q_n)$ is the function of occurrence of the top event. q_i is the probability of occurrence of the event i.

The first expression to be set is Q_{Sys} as function of q_i. It is derived with respect to the corresponding variable. The procedure to find the expression is:

1. To simplify the logical expression that defines the system using the Boolean algebra rules. This allows for obtaining a logical expression given by the sum of the MCSs.

2. The probability of occurrence of the top event is the probability of the union of these MCSs, calculated using the principle of inclusion-exclusion (see ANNEX XIII).

3. The principle of idempotent will be applied in those terms that include probability of intersections and MOEs, i.e., the terms that contain factors x_i^n, being a linear function Q_{Sys} for each q_i.

The Birnbaum IM can be expressed as a difference of conditional probabilities of occurrence. It is defined by Eq. (2.4).

$$I^{\text{Birn}} = P\left(\frac{Q_{\text{Sys}}}{q_i}\right) - P\left(\frac{Q_{\text{Sys}}}{\overline{q_i}}\right) \tag{2.4}$$

where Q_{Sys} is the probability of occurrence of the top event; q_i is the probability of occurrence of the basic event i; $\overline{q_i}$ is the probability of non-occurrence of the basic event i.

The derivative of the expression (2.4) can be written as follows:

$$I^{\text{Birn}} = \frac{\partial Q_{\text{Sys}}}{\partial q_i} = \frac{Q_{\text{Sys}}(1_i, q) - Q_{\text{Sys}}(0_i, q)}{1 - 0}$$

It can be also expressed as:

$$I^{\text{Birn}} = Q_{\text{Sys}}(1_i, q) - Q_{\text{Sys}}(0_i, q) \tag{2.5}$$

where

$$Q_{\text{Sys}}(1_i, q) = Q_{\text{Sys}}(q_1, q_2, \ldots, q_{i-1}, 1, q_{i+1}, \ldots, q_n) \tag{2.6}$$

$$Q_{\text{Sys}}(0_i, q) = Q_{\text{Sys}}(q_1, q_2, \ldots, q_{i-1}, 0, q_{i+1}, \ldots, q_n) \tag{2.7}$$

Example 2.3 presents a simple case study where the Birnbaum IM is calculated step by step.

Example 2.3

A system is composed by two events A and B, linked by an OR gate. The logical function is $f = A + B$. The probabilities of occurrence for each event are $q_A = 0.1$ and $q_B = 0.2$.

Q_{Sys} is provided by the union of both events:

$$Q_{\text{Sys}} = P(A \cup B) = P(A) + P(B) - P(A \cap B) = q_A + q_B - q_A q_B$$

Employing Eq. (2.5):

$$I^{\text{Birn}} = \frac{\partial Q_{\text{Sys}}}{\partial q_i} = 1 - q_B = 1 - 0.2 = 0.8$$

Considering Eq. (2.5) and that the event A has occurred, the probability of occurrence of the top event is 1 because $f = 1 + B = 1$. If the event A has not occurred, the probability of occurrence of the top event is the probability of occurrence of B, because of $f = 0 + B = B$.

$$Q_{\text{Sys}}(1_A, q) = 1 + q_B - q_B = 1$$

$$Q_{\text{Sys}}(0_A, q) = 0 + q_B - 0 = q_B$$

$$I_A^{\text{Birn}} = Q_{\text{Sys}}(1_A, \boldsymbol{q}) - Q_{\text{Sys}}(0_A, \boldsymbol{q}) = 1 - q_B = 1 - 0.2 = 0.8$$

Employing Eqs. (2.6), (2.7):

$$Q_{\text{Sys}}(1_A, \boldsymbol{q}) = 1 + q_B - q_B = 1$$

$$Q_{\text{Sys}}(0_A, \boldsymbol{q}) = 0 + q_B - 0 = q_B$$

$$I_A^{\text{Birn}} = Q_{\text{Sys}}(1_A, \boldsymbol{q}) - Q_{\text{Sys}}(0_A, \boldsymbol{q}) = 1 - q_B = 1 - 0.2 = 0.8$$

2.3.3 Criticality

A disadvantage of the Birnbaum IM is that it does not consider the probability of occurrence of the event analyzed. This can lead to assigning a high importance to rare events.[2] The *Criticality* IM can be used to correct it.[52] This measure modulates the Birnbaum IM using a factor to measure the weight of the event in the system that considers the occurrence probability of the event. The definition of the Criticality IM for a certain event is expressed by Eq. (2.8).

$$I_i^{\text{Crit}} = \left(\frac{q_i}{Q_{\text{Sys}}} \right) \cdot \left(\frac{\partial Q_{\text{Sys}}}{\partial q_i} \right) = \left(\frac{q_i}{Q_{\text{Sys}}} \right) \cdot I_i^{\text{Birn}} \qquad (2.8)$$

2.3.4 Structural Importance

Starting from the definition of the Birnbaum IM given by Eq. (2.5), and following the Lambert's method,[52] the *Structural* IM is defined as:

$$I_i^{\text{Struct}} = Q_{\text{Sys}}(1_i, 1/2) - Q_{\text{Sys}}(0_i, 1/2) \qquad (2.9)$$

where

$$Q_{\text{Sys}}(1_i, 1/2) = Q_{\text{Sys}}\left(q_1 = \frac{1}{2}, \dots, q_{i-1} = \frac{1}{2}, q_i = 1, q_{i+1} = \frac{1}{2}, \dots, q_n = 1/2 \right)$$
$$(2.9\text{a})$$

$$Q_{\text{Sys}}(1_i, 1/2) = Q_{\text{Sys}}\left(q_1 = \frac{1}{2}, \dots, q_{i-1} = \frac{1}{2}, q_i = 1, q_{i+1} = \frac{1}{2}, \dots, q_n = 1/2 \right)$$
$$(2.9\text{b})$$

2.3.5 AND Method

This method establishes the importance of each basic event by counting the number of *AND* gates on the path from the event analyzed to the top

---

[2] The *rare events* are those events whose probability of occurrence is very low.

event.[53] It is applicable to a LDT with events whose probabilities of occurrence are unknown, being the most important advantage of this method.

This approach considers that the events under AND gates are less "important" than the events under OR gates, due to a state 1 at the output of an AND gate requires all the input events to occur. Assuming double-input gates, each event needs at least other event at the same level to occur. The events with a lower number of AND gates have more priority, i.e., more importance.

Events will be ordered according to the number of AND gates in the path to the top event that can be set by the following steps:

- To count the number of AND gates in the path to the top event for each basic event.
- To classify the events into categories with regard to the number of AND gates to the top event.
- Events in the same category will be decreasingly ordered considering their probability of occurrence.
- The events that are closer to the top are more important if there are events with the same probabilities being in the same category.
- The same importance will be assigned to the events that are in the same category and are linked by an OR gate.
- If there is any repeated event located in different places of the LDT, the most restrictive will be considered to determine its importance.

2.3.6 Other Importance Measures

- The *Barlow-Proschan* IM provides the number of cases in which the top event occurs by the occurrence of the event i in the period $[0, t]$. It is given by Eq. (2.10).

$$I_i^{BP} = \int_0^t \left[Q_{Sys}(1_i, \mathbf{q}) - Q_{Sys}(o_i, \mathbf{q}) \right] \cdot w_i(t) dt \qquad (2.10)$$

- The *Risk Achievement Worth (RAW)* is an IM that provides a measure of the degradation of the system assuming the occurrence of a certain event.[54] It is defined as:

$$RAW_i = \frac{P\left(\dfrac{Q_{Sys}}{x_i}\right)}{Q_{Sys}} \qquad (2.11)$$

It is calculated normally dividing the sum of the probabilities of the MCSs containing the basic event i, assuming a probability of 1 (occurrence) for this event, and the total probability of the top event:

$$RAW_i = \frac{\sum_{j=1}^{m} P\left(e_{j,\,q_i=1}^i\right)}{P\left(\bigcup_{k=1}^n e_k\right)} \qquad (2.12)$$

- The *Risk Reduction Worth* (*RRW*) measures how much the probability of the top event decreases when the event i does not occur.[54] It identifies those basic events that cause the greatest reductions in the probability of the top event when their probabilities of occurrence decrease. It is calculated by Eq. (2.13).

$$RRW_i = \frac{Q_{Sys}}{P\left(\dfrac{Q_{Sys}}{x_i}\right)} \qquad (2.13)$$

It is also calculated by dividing the probability of the top event and the sum of the probabilities of all the MCSs, assuming that the probability of occurrence of the event i is 0.

$$RAW_i = \frac{P\left(\bigcup_{k=1}^n e_k\right)}{\sum_{j=1}^{m} P\left(e_{j,\,q_i=0}^i\right)} \qquad (2.14)$$

2.4 SENSITIVITY ANALYSIS AND UNCERTAINTY ANALYSIS

The *sensitivity analysis* aims to measure changes in the system caused by variations in the probabilities of the events. The effects on the top event are evaluated when the probabilities of the basic events change.

A sensitivity analysis can answer the following questions:
1. What are the weaknesses of the system?
2. How do variations in the input parameters affect the results?
3. What event is better to invest in to improve the DM?

The system is assumed to be sensitive to a particular event when a variation in the probability of this event leads to the system to vary considerably.

An uncertainty analysis is done to analyze the variations of the probability of occurrence of the top event due to the dispersion on the data of certain basic events. Statistics and probabilistic techniques can be used to perform this type of analysis.

2.5 COMMON CAUSE OCCURRENCES

The logical model considers that the basic events located under the same gate are independent. This is a limitation because possible implicit dependencies between them may not be taken into account.

In case of two independent basic events, the probability of the intersection is:

$$P(A \cap B) = P(A) \cdot P(B)$$

However, if both events are dependent, then:

$$P(A \cap B) > P(A) \cdot P(B)$$

Therefore, the contribution to the probability of the top event will be greater when there are some dependencies, and they must be studied to obtain a representative logical model of the system.

The *common cause occurrences* (*CCOs*) are generated when two or more events occur simultaneously, or in a relatively short period of time, due to a "common cause."[55]

The CCOs are not included in the initial model of LDT because they are usually caused by dependencies that are difficult to identify a priori. In this case, previous qualitative analysis of the initial LDT is required to identify them.

According to *Mosleh* (1998), the dependencies can be classified into[56]:

- *Endogenous to the system.* The occurrence of a certain event is affected by the occurrence of another event. In this type of dependencies there are several subclasses:
  - *Functional requirement dependence.* The condition of a specific event determines whether the occurrence of an event *B* is required. There are four cases: the occurrence (or nonoccurrence) of *B* is required when the event *A* occurs, and the occurrence (or nonoccurrence) of *B* is required when the event *A* does not occur.
  - *Functional occurrence between events.* The occurrence of a certain event *A* may cause the occurrence of an event *B*.
  - *Cascade of occurrences.* The occurrence of one event may cause the occurrence of several events.
  - *Other.* There are other endogenous dependencies because of combinations of the above dependencies.
- *Exogenous to the system.* They are considered as nonfunctional features of the system, being:
  - *Physical and environmental dependencies.* They can be: external environmental conditions (fire, storm, flood, earthquake, etc.) or; extreme

physical operating conditions (pressure, temperature, humidity, vibration, etc.). It includes conditions caused by the occurrence of an event that creates an abnormal environment.

- Dependencies due to human factors.

The CCOs are often used to model systems redundancies[3] because their probabilities increase when there are multiple events with the same specifications. A simple example is presented to demonstrate the importance of the CCOs. For this purpose, a subsystem composed of three redundant events is considered (Fig. 2.2). The logical model is presented in reference.[57]

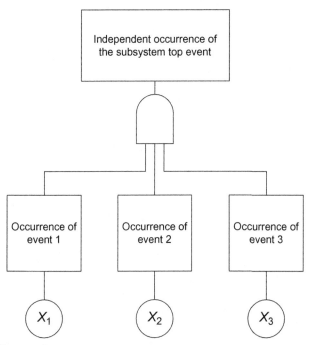

Fig. 2.2 LDT example.

Considering that the probabilities of occurrence of the events are (Fig. 2.2):

$$q_1 = q_2 = q_3 = q = 10^{-3}$$

---

[3] The *redundancies* are defined as a set of identical elements that can perform the same function. They can cause the probability of occurrence of the top event to decrease, e.g., the use of four engines on a plane.

The probability that the events occur independently is given by:

$$Q_{indep} = q_1 = q_2 = q_3 = q^3 = 10^{-9}$$

The probability that the events occur at the same time is very low (one in a billion).

Considering the case where the possibility of a CCO for the three components, and 1% are due to a common cause, the probability that the components occur because of a CCO is:

$$Q_{CCO} = 1\%(q) = 10^{-2} \times 10^{-3} = 10^{-5}$$

The probability of occurrence due to CCO is 10^4 times bigger than the probability of occurrence of the independent events. It is demonstrated that the CCOs have a great importance in the LDT modeling. Fig. 2.3 shows how to include CCOs. The probability of occurrence of the top event including the CCO is given by:

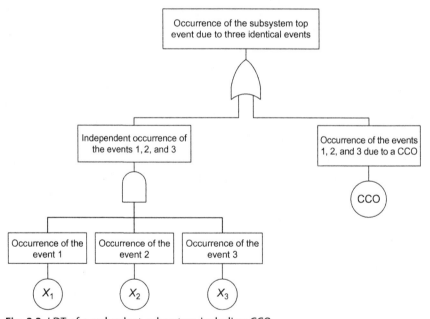

Fig. 2.3 LDT of a redundant subsystem including CCO.

$$Q_{Sys} = Q_{indep} + Q_{CCO} - Q_{indep}Q_{CCO} = 10^{-5} + 10^{-9} - 10^{-14} \cong 10^{-5}$$

The logical models must be chosen once the CCO has been identified. The factor β method is the easiest to model the CCOs. This method considers that the total rate of occurrence of an event can be decomposed into the following two rates:

$$\lambda = \lambda_{\text{indep}} + \lambda_{\text{CCO}}$$

β is defined as the quotient between the rate of occurrence of an event that corresponds to a CCO and the global rate of occurrence.

$$\beta = \frac{\lambda_{\text{CCO}}}{\lambda}$$

Other methods used to model CCOs are: the *alpha factor method, multiple greek letters method (MGL)*, etc.

2.6 LIMITATIONS OF CONVENTIONAL METHODS FOR TREE ANALYSIS

The methods present some drawbacks in the evaluation, which are mainly due to:
- *LDT size*

The number of MCSs (PIs, for coherent structures) increases exponentially with the number of basic events, being an NP-complete problem. Therefore, the calculation of the probability of the top event is also an exponential problem.

Poincaré's formula is used to achieve the probability of the union of the PIs and to address the calculation of the probability of the top event. However, this formula does not allow operating with large LDTs. This computational problem requires approximations to simplify the problem, where they compute only the most relevant PIs.
- *Complexity of the LDT*

The redundancies increase the computational cost because it is necessary to make simplifications of the logical expression. Idempotent and absorption rules are used to eliminate redundant terms.

Large combinations of AND/OR gates cause difficult calculations and increase the computational cost.
- *Computational limitations*
  - Processor speed
  - Memory size
  - Programming language
  - Etc.

CHAPTER 3

Binary Decision Diagrams

3.1 INTRODUCTION

BDDs are data structures used to represent Boolean functions. They were proposed in the 70s by *Akers* as models for DM.[58] Later, they were popularized by *Randal E. Bryant*[59] who represented these structures in its canonical form. This form establishes a set of constrains and provides great advantages to operate with the BDDs.

An *ordered binary decision diagram (OBDD)* is a BDD where all the variables are ordered.[60]

A *reduced ordered binary decision diagram (ROBDD)* is an OBDD where certain principles have been applied to get a smaller BDD. It contains neither repetitive sub-logical decision trees (LDTs) nor redundant vertex. All the variables must be ordered, and this order cannot be changed during the generation of these diagrams. A ROBDD is associated with a set of algorithms.[61]

Nowadays, the BDDs are applied to a large number of cases, e.g., to represent LDTs in the field of DM because they are a useful tool to operate with Boolean expressions.[62,63]

The main advantage of the BDDs is the possibility of evaluating the top event using implicit formulas. It avoids the exponential growth of the number of PIs. The BDDs use less computational memory than the explicit representations for representing Boolean functions.

3.1.1 Definition

A BDD is a *directed acyclic graph (DAG)* that simulates a logical function. It is a structure **G(V, N)**, composed by vertices (**V**) that are connected by branches (**N**). Each vertex can be a terminal or a nonterminal vertex:

- *Nonterminal vertex:* It is a vertex associated with a basic event. A nonterminal vertex is followed by two branches: 1 if the event occurs; 0 if the event does not occur.

The nodes under a nonterminal vertex are called "sons" of that vertex. Therefore, each nonterminal vertex has two "sons": the upper one and the lower one. The function associated with a nonterminal vertex is given by the *Shannon's* theorem (Eq. 3.1):

$$f_v(e_1, e_2, ..., e_i, ...e_n) = e_i f_{low(v)}(e_1, e_2, ..., 1, ...e_n) + \overline{e_i} f_{up(v)}(e_1, e_2, ..., 0, ...e_n)$$

$$(3.1)$$

where e_i is the logical variables: Occurrence $(e_i = 1)$ or nonoccurrence $(e_i = 0)$. $f_{low}(v)$ is the lower "son" of the vertex **V** that corresponds to the branch *if* (case $e_i = 1$). $f_{up}(v)$ is the upper "son" of the vertex **V**, that corresponds to the branch *else* (case $e_i = 0$).

A special nonterminal vertex is the vertex located at the top of the graph. This is not a "son" of any other vertex. This vertex is called the "root vertex" of the *BDD*.

- A *terminal vertex* is a node that is located at the end of a path and is not followed by any branch, i.e., it does not have "sons." The terminal vertices only can be associated with values 1 and 0 that correspond to the possible condition of the system, where:

$$f_v = 1, \quad \text{when } (V) = 1$$
$$f_v = 0, \quad \text{when } (V) = 0$$

The nonterminal vertices usually have sons, or at least one, that represent logical expressions. However, the two "sons" of every terminal vertex are directly logical values.[64]

All the paths of a BDD begin in the "root vertex" and end in "a terminal vertex." Fig. 3.1 shows an example of BDD.

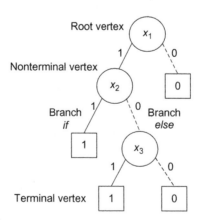

Fig. 3.1 BDD structure.

3.1.2 Shannon's Theorem and ITE Sentences

The construction of a BDD is based on the recursive expansion of a digital function, or structure function, using Shannon's theorem. It is given by Eq. (3.1a).

$$f = x_i f_{xi=1} + \overline{x_i} f_{xi=1} = x_i f_1 + \overline{x_i} f_2 \tag{3.1a}$$

where the logical functions f_1, f_2 are "sons" of x_i.

A logical expression can be expressed using *If-Then-Else* (*ITE*) control expressions. Eq. (3.1a) is equivalent to:

$$\text{If } x_i \text{ Then } f_1 \text{ Else } f_2$$

This control expression will be denoted as $ite(e_1, f_1, f_2)$. Therefore, each *Shannon's expansion* can be noted as Eq. (3.2).

$$f = ite(e_i, f_1, f_2) \tag{3.2}$$

and it can be represented graphically as shown by Fig. 3.2.

Fig. 3.2 BDD for *ite*(x_i, f_1, f_2).

The left branch in Fig. 3.2 is associated with the state 1 (occurrence of x_i), and the right branch is associated with a state 0 (nonoccurrence of x_i). This notation will be used in the following figures.

A logical variable can be expressed by Eq. (3.3) and it is represented in Fig. 3.3.

$$x_i = ite(x_i, 1, 0) \tag{3.3}$$

Fig. 3.3 ITE notation for a variable.

3.2 BDDs RULES AND OPERATIONS

The rules that will be used in the conversion from LDT to BDD and to simplify the BDDs are presented in this section.

3.2.1 Operation Rules

Assuming that $F = ite(x, F_1, F_2)$ and $G = ite(x, G_1, G_2)$, then:

(a) $x < y$:

$$F\langle op\rangle G = ite(x, F_1\langle op\rangle G, F_2\langle op\rangle G) \qquad (3.4)$$

(b) $x = y$:

$$F\langle op\rangle G = ite(x, F_1\langle op\rangle G_1, F_2\langle op\rangle G_2) \qquad (3.5)$$

(c) $x > y$:

$$F\langle op\rangle G = ite(y, F\langle op\rangle G_1, F\langle op\rangle G_2) \qquad (3.6)$$

The operator $<op>$ indicates a generic logical operation (OR, AND,...). It is an advantage with respect to other structures that require different algorithms to implement each type of operation. If one of the expressions would be a logical value, then:

$$F\langle op\rangle 1 = 1, \quad \text{if } \langle op\rangle = OR \qquad (3.7)$$
$$F\langle op\rangle 1 = F, \quad \text{if } \langle op\rangle = AND \qquad (3.8)$$
$$F\langle op\rangle 0 = F, \quad \text{if } \langle op\rangle = OR \qquad (3.9)$$
$$F\langle op\rangle 0 = 0, \quad \text{if } \langle op\rangle = AND \qquad (3.10)$$

3.2.2 Reduction Rules

The next rules are used to reduce the BDD graphs:

- *Rule 1: Elimination of duplicate terminal vertices.* Duplicate terminal vertices are eliminated leaving only two terminal nodes (with value 1 and with value 0). The terminal branches are redirected to the undeleted terminal vertices.
- *Rule 2: Elimination of duplicate nonterminal vertices.* If there are two nonterminal vertices u and v that belong to the same variable and if $f_{low}(u) = f_{low}(v)$ and $f_{upp}(u) = f_{upp}(v)$, one vertex is eliminated and its branches are redirected to the other vertex.
- *Rule 3: Elimination of redundant vertices.* If there is a nonterminal vertex whose "sons" are $f_{low}(v) = f_{upp}(v)$, it is eliminated and its branches are redirected to the "son" vertex.

Example 3.1
The logical function $f = x_2 x_3 + x_1 x_3 + x_1 x_2 x_3$ is given, represented by Table 3.1.

Table 3.1 Truth table for $f = x_2 x_3 + x_1 x_3 + x_1 x_2 x_3$

x_1	x_2	x_3	f
0	0	0	0
0	0	1	0
0	1	0	0
0	1	1	1
1	0	0	0
1	0	1	1
1	1	0	0
1	1	1	1

Table 3.1 shows the graph associated with the truth table in Table 3.1.

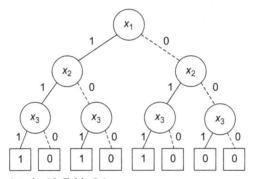

Fig. 3.4 BDD associated with Table 3.1.

The duplicate terminal vertices are eliminated to reduce the graph given in Fig. 3.4, obtaining Fig. 3.5.

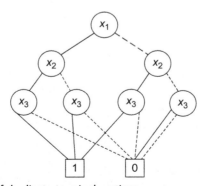

Fig. 3.5 Elimination of duplicate terminal vertices.

The next step to a further reduction of the graph in Fig. 3.5 is to eliminate the nonterminal vertices, obtaining the graph given in Fig. 3.6

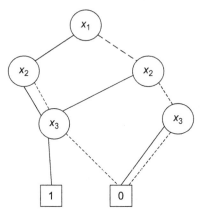

Fig. 3.6 Elimination of duplicate nonterminal vertices.

Finally, the last reduction step will be associated with the elimination of redundant vertices, where Fig. 3.7 is obtained.

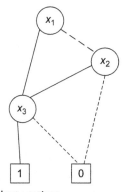

Fig. 3.7 Elimination of redundant vertices.

Therefore, the function $f = x_2 x_3 + x_1 x_3 + x_1 x_2 x_3$ can be expressed as $f = x_1 x_3 + x_2 x_3$.

3.2.3 Gate Transformation Rules

(a) OR gates

Firstly, the ITE format for a logical sum will be generated. The logical variables can be expressed as:

$$x_1 = ite\,(x_1, 1, 0)$$
$$x_2 = ite\,(x_2, 1, 0)$$

Considering the order $x_1 < x_2$, the logical sum of these variables according to Eq. (3.4) is:

$$x_1 + x_2 = ite(x_1, 1, 0) + ite(x_2, 1, 0)$$
$$= ite(x_1, 1 + ite(x_2, 1, 0), 0 + ite(x_2, 1, 0)) = ite(x_1, 1, ite(x_2, 1, 0))$$

It is represented graphically as shown in Fig. 3.8.

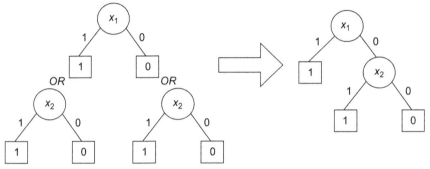

Fig. 3.8 Logical sum of two variables.

Fig. 3.8 shows that if at least one of the inputs is true, then there will be a "1" in the output. Therefore, the logical sum of two variables is noted as in Eq. (3.11).

$$x_1 + x_2 = ite(x_1, 1, x_2) \tag{3.11}$$

The logical sum of two logical functions expressed in the ITE format is given by Eq. (3.12) (see Fig. 3.9).

$$f_{or} = ite(f_1, 1, f_2) \tag{3.12}$$

$$f_{OR} = f_1 + f_2$$

$$f_1 \quad f_2$$

Fig. 3.9 Graph associated to Eq. (3.12).

This is equivalent to the BDD shown in Fig. 3.10.

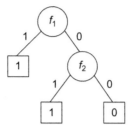

Fig. 3.10 BDD for the logical sum (OR) of two logical functions.

(b) AND gates

The ITE format for a logical product is generated according to Eq. (3.4). Assuming the order $x_1 < x_2$:

$$x_1 x_2 = ite(x_1, 1, 0) \cdot ite(x_2, 1, 0) = ite(x_1, 1 \cdot ite(x_2, 1, 0), 0 \cdot ite(x_2, 1, 0))$$
$$= ite(x_1, ite(x_2, 1, 0), 0)$$

This can be represented graphically by Fig. 3.11.

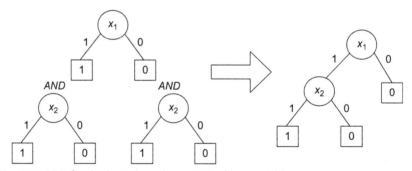

Fig. 3.11 BDD for the logical product (AND) of two variables.

Being

$$x_1 x_2 = ite(x_1, x_2, 0) \tag{3.13}$$

The logical product of two logical functions (see Fig. 3.12) expressed in the ITE format is given by Eq. (3.14).

$$f_{\text{AND}} = ite(f_1, f_2, 0) \tag{3.14}$$

This is equivalent to the BDD presented in Fig. 3.13

$$f_{AND} = f_1 \cdot f_2$$

Fig. 3.12 Graph associated to Eq. (3.14).

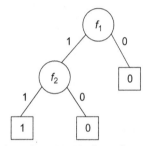

Fig. 3.13 BDD for the logical product (AND) of two logical functions.

3.2.4 Reduction Rules

If M and N are logical variables, then:

$$ite(1, M, N) = M \tag{3.15a}$$

$$ite(0, M, N) = N \tag{3.15b}$$

$$ite(M, M, N) = M \tag{3.15c}$$

$$ite(1, M, N) = M \tag{3.15d}$$

$$ite(M, N, N) = N \tag{3.15e}$$

3.2.5 Expansion Rules

$$ite((M, N_1, N_2), N_3, N_4) = ite(M, ite(N_1, N_2, N_3, N_4, ite(N_2, N_3, N_4))) \tag{3.16}$$

3.2.6 Absorption Rules

$$ite(M, ite(M, N_1, N_2), N_3) = ite(M, N_1, N_3) \tag{3.17a}$$

$$ite(M, N_1, ite(M, N_2, N_3)) = ite(M, N_1, N_3) \tag{3.17b}$$

3.2.7 Relations to Change the Order

Each vertex of a LDT has an associated index. The following relationships have to be applied when a new variable order is set in the reordering phase of the BDD:

If $index(M_1) < index(M) \leq index(M_2)$:

$$ite(M, M_1, M_2) = ite(M_1, ite(M, 1, M_2), ite(M, 0, M_2)) \qquad (3.18a)$$

If $index(M_2) < index(M) \leq index(M_1)$:

$$ite(M, M_1, M_2) = ite(M_2, ite(M, M_1, 1), ite(M, M_1, 0)) \qquad (3.18b)$$

If $index(M_1) \leq index(M_2) < index(M)$:

$$ite(M, M_1, M_2) = ite(M_1, ite(M_2, 1, M), ite(M_2, ite(M, 0, 1), 0)) \qquad (3.18c)$$

If $index(M_2) < index(M) < index(M_1)$:

$$ite(M, M_1, M_2) = ite(M_2, ite(M_1, 1, ite(M, 0, 1)), ite(M_1, M, 0)) \qquad (3.18d)$$

3.3 VARIABLE RANKING

Different BDDs can be generated from the same LDT depending on the way of applying the Shannon's expansions. The size of the resulting BDD will strongly depend on the order assigned to the basic events. A nonoptimal order of the variables can produce an exponential growth of the BDD size. The selection of the variable ordering is one of the most important problems in the use of BDDs, and many researchers have focused their efforts on search effective ranking methods.

3.3.1 Importance of the Variable Ordering

An inefficient variable ranking usually produce a large BDD. Different rankings generate different BDD sizes. Fig. 3.14 shows a LDT that corresponds to the logical function: $f = x_1 + x_2 + x_3 + x_4$. It will be analyzed for the importance of a right variable ordering.

- The conversion from LDT to BDD is carried out according to the ranking, e.g., ranking

$$x_1 < x_2 < x_3 < x_4$$

$$G_2 = ite(x_2, 1, 0) + ite(x_3, 1, 0) = ite(x_2, 1 + ite(x_3, 1, 0), 0 + ite(x_3, 1, 0))$$
$$= ite(x_2, 1, ite(x_3, 1, 0))$$

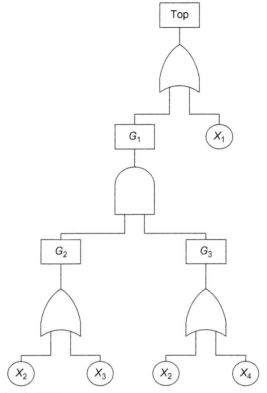

Fig. 3.14 Example of a LTD.

$$G_3 = ite(x_2, 1, 0) + ite(x_4, 1, 0) = ite(x_2, 1 + ite(x_4, 1, 0), 0 + ite(x_4, 1, 0))$$
$$= ite(x_2, 1, ite(x_4, 1, 0))$$

$$G_1 = ite(x_2, 1, ite(x_3, 1, 0)) \cdot ite(x_2, 1, ite(x_4, 1, 0))$$
$$= ite(x_2, 1 \cdot 1, ite(x_3, 1, 0) \cdot ite(x_4, 1, 0))$$
$$= ite(x_2, 1, ite(x_3, 1 \cdot ite(x_4, 1, 0), 0 \cdot ite(x_4, 1, 0)))$$
$$= ite(x_2, 1, ite(x_3, x_4, 0))$$

$$Top = ite(x_1, 1, 0) + ite(x_2, 1, ite(x_3, x_4, 0))$$
$$= ite(x_1, 1 + ite(x_2, 1, ite(x_3, x_4, 0))0 + ite(x_2, 1, ite(x_3, x_4, 0)))$$
$$= ite(x_1, 1, ite(x_3, x_4, 0))$$

If the logical function is simplified, then:

$$f(x_1, x_2, x_3, x_4) = (x_2 + x_3)(x_2 + x_4) + x_1 = x_2 + x_2x_3 + x_2x_4 + x_3x_4 + x_1$$
$$= x_2 + x_3x_4 + x_1$$

Therefore, the MCSs are:

$$MCS_1 = x_1$$
$$MCS_2 = x_2$$
$$MCS_3 = x_3 x_4$$

The *BDD* is obtained employing expansion rules according to the ranking shown in Fig. 3.15.

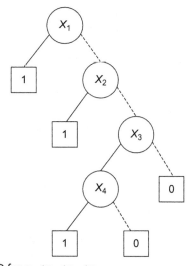

Fig. 3.15 Resulting *BBD* for $x_1 < x_2 < x_3 < x_4$.

$$f = ite(x_1, 1, (x_2 + x_3)(x_2 + x_4)) = ite(x_1, 1, ite(x_2, 1, x_3 x_4))$$
$$= ite(x_1, 1, ite(x_2, 1, ite(x_3, x_4, 0)))$$

A different variable ranking has been taken into account in the following example:

Ranking $x_4 < x_3 < x_2 < x_1$:

The expressions obtained using the ITE formats are:

$$G_2 = ite(x_2, 1, 0) + ite(x_3, 1, 0) = ite(x_3, 1 + ite(x_2, 1, 0), 0 + ite(x_2, 1, 0))$$
$$= ite(x_3, 1, ite(x_2, 1, 0))$$

$$G_3 = ite(x_2, 1, 0) + ite(x_4, 1, 0) = ite(x_4, 1 + ite(x_2, 1, 0), 0 + ite(x_2, 1, 0))$$
$$= ite(x_4, 1, ite(x_2, 1, 0))$$

$$G_1 = ite(x_3, 1, ite(x_2, 1, 0)) \cdot ite(x_4, 1, ite(x_2, 1, 0))$$
$$= ite(x_4, 1 \cdot ite(x_3, 1, ite(x_2, 1, 0)), ite(x_2, 1, 0) \cdot ite(x_3, 1, ite(x_2, 1, 0)))$$
$$= ite(x_4, ite(x_3, 1, ite(x_2, 1, 0), ite(x_3, 1 \cdot ite(x_2, 1, 0),$$
$$ite(x_2, 1, 0) \cdot ite(x_2, 1, 0))))$$
$$= ite(x_4, ite(x_3, 1, ite(x_2, 1, 0), ite(x_3, ite(x_2, 1, 10), ite(x_2, 1, 0))))$$

$$Top = ite(x_1, 1, 0) + ite(x_4, ite(x_3, 1, ite(x_2, 1, 0)), ite(x_3, ite(x_2, 1, 0)))$$
$$= ite(x_4, ite(x_3, 1, ite(x_2, 1, 0)) + ite(x_1, 1, 0), ite(x_3, ite(x_2, 1, 0),$$
$$ite(x_2, 1, 0) + ite(x_1, 1, 0)))$$
$$= ite(x_4, ite(x_3, 1, ite(x_2, 1, 0) + ite(x_1, 1, 0)), ite(x_3, ite(x_2, 1, 0)$$
$$+ ite(x_1, 1, 0), ite(x_2, 1, 0) + ite(x_1, 1, 0)))$$
$$= ite(x_4, ite(x_3, 1, ite(x_2, 1, ite(x_1, 1, 0))), ite(x_3, ite(x_2, 1, ite(x_1, 1, 0)),$$
$$ite(x_2, 1, ite(x_1, 1, 0))))$$

The *BDD* can be represented as follows:

$$f = ite(x_4, (x_2 + x_3) + x_1, (x_2 + x_3)x_2 + x_1)$$
$$= ite(x_4, ite(x_3, 1, x_2 + x_1), ite(x_3, x_2 + x_1, x_2 + x_1))$$
$$= ite(x_4, ite(x_3, 1, ite(x_2, 1, x_1)), ite(x_3, ite(x_2, 1, x_1), ite(x_2, 1, x_1)))$$

Fig. 3.16 shows that the ranking $x_4 < x_3 < x_2 < x_1$ is not efficient due to the BDD obtained being larger than the BDD presented in Fig. 3.14. This ranking produces seven nonterminal vertices, and the previous one only produces 4 nonterminal vertices. The BDD presented in Fig. 3.15 has the minimum size that can be obtained for the logical function of the example.

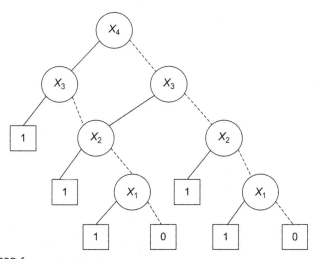

Fig. 3.16 *BBD* for $x_4 < x_3 < x_2 < x_1$.

3.3.2 Ranking Methods

The problem of finding the optimal variable ranking is NP–complete and it cannot be solved in a reasonable time. Heuristic methods are widely used to find an efficient ranking. These methods do not provide an optimal solution, but they provide a good one. The main methods are:

- *Topological Heuristic Methods:* They are the simplest methods and the easiest to implement. No calculations are performed in these methods, but a procedure to read the LDT is chosen and the variables are ranked in the order in which they are found.
  - *Top-Down Left-Right (TDLR):* The LDT is read from the top to bottom, and from left to right. The ranking is generated according to the order in which the events are found.[65] An example is shown in Fig. 3.17.

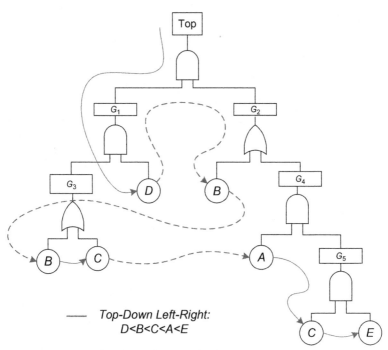

Fig. 3.17 Top-Down Left-Right ranking method.

  - *Depth First Search (DFS):* The LDT is read from top to bottom, and in each level the left LDTs are read firstly. An example is shown in Fig. 3.18.

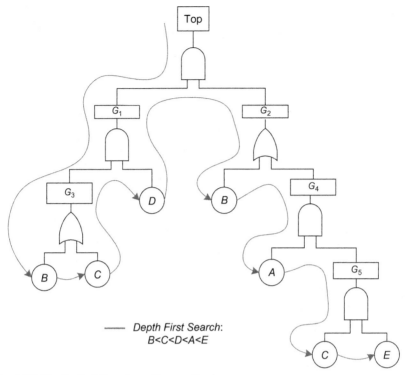

Fig. 3.18 Depth First Search ranking method.

- • *Breadth-First Search (BFS):* The LDT is read from left to right, and the events are ranked according to the order that they are found. It must be stated that if a repeated event is found, then it must be ignored.
- • *Weights method, or Minato's heuristic*[66]: Unitary weights are assigned to the nonterminal vertices, and the weight of each "father" will be the sum of the weights of its "sons." Finally, the events are reordered in decreasing weights. There are some variants of this heuristic method, such as *Weight-Op* that assigns different weight values in function of the logical gates.[67] An example is shown in Fig. 3.19.
- • *Method of flows*[68]: Flow values are assigned to each branch of the LDT. The root node that is assigned a unitary flow, and the flow values are propagated downward. The flow of a "son" depends on the sum of the flows of the "fathers." Finally, the events are reordered in decreasing weights.
- • *Method of fathers*[69]: The total number of "fathers" is counted for each variable. The "sons" are ranked in descending order of number of "fathers."

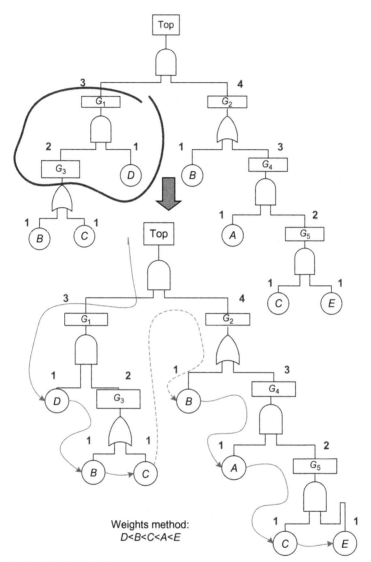

Fig. 3.19 Weights' method.

- *Level Method*[70]: This method is not so simple and direct. It makes a difference between the basic events depending on their location, i.e., it is directly related with the number of gates that are above them. The MOEs are listed first when there are events in the same level.
- *Heuristic method based on the structural importance*[71]: This ranking method is based on the Structural Birnbaum Measure. This measure can be achieved using Eq. (2.6), where the probability of occurrence of the events is

required. It is a difficult task when the LDT is large. *Bartlett* (2001) proposes an alternative to achieve an approximation of this measure.[71]

1. Generate a list of events using TDLR method.

2. Choose an event *i* and follow the next steps:

  2.1. Consider the probability of the event *i* as 1, and the probabilities of the rest of events as 1/2.

  2.2. Set the probability of the event *i* as 0, and the probabilities of the rest of events as 1/2.

The gates that only have basic events are chosen. The output probabilities of these gates are achieved:

(a) If it is an *AND* gate: Πq_i

(b) If it is an OR gate: $1 - \Pi(1 - q_i)$

(c) The probabilities obtained in steps 2.1 and 2.2 are obtained.

The AND method, explained in Section 2.3.5, can be also used as a ranking method.[53]

Bartlett's method provides an appropriate importance analysis when there is much uncertainty in the input data. In general, topologic heuristics methods are not robust. Although they produce good results, sometimes they are unpredictable and produce inefficient rankings. These methods can become more robust by applying some restrictions (weights, flows, etc.).

3.3.3 A Novel Ranking Method

A new ranking method has been defined by the authors of this book.[72] It aims to reduce the size of the BDDs taking into account the following considerations:

• Each logical gate of the LDT needs an appropriate weighting.

• An importance is assigned to each event evaluating the multiplication of the weighting of the gates from the event considered to the Top Event.

• The basic events are sorted in decreasing values of importance.

• The weighting of each logical gate will depend on its nature (OR or AND gates), and the number of events under the logical gate.

If there are "*n*" events through an AND logical gate, the event could only be extended through the gate if all the "*n*" events occur, i.e., only 1 state of the 2^n possible states will cause the occurrence of the "father event."

If there are n events through an AND logical gate, the occurrence of the "father" event of that gate could only occur if all the n events are given, i.e., there is only one state of the 2^n possible states that will cause the occurrence of the "father" event. Therefore, the weight assigned to an AND logical gate will be:

$$P_{\text{and}}(n) = \frac{1}{2^n}$$

The "father" event of an OR gate will occur in all cases when any of the events is not 0, i.e., only one of the 2^n states will not cause the occurrence of the "father" event, and consequently, the occurrence of the top will not be caused by these events. The mentioned state is the one in which the state of all the events is 0. Therefore, the OR logic gate weighting is:

$$P_{\text{or}}(n) = \frac{2^n - 1}{2^n}$$

The new approach for ranking the events is summarized in Fig. 3.20.

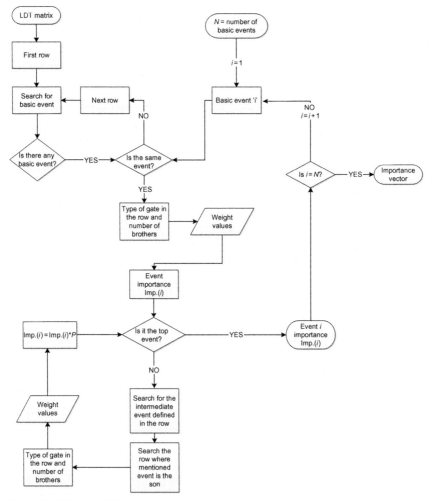

Fig. 3.20 Scheme of the new approach for ranking events.

Fig. 3.21 shows a LDT as an example for ranking the event employing the new approach (Fig. 3.20).

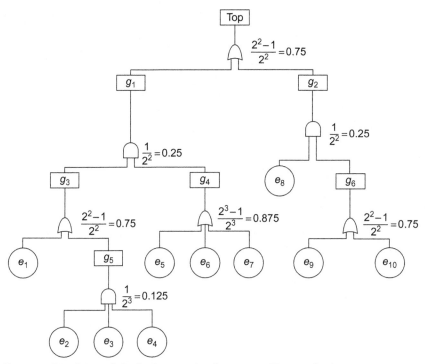

Fig. 3.21 Weighting of the logic gates by the new ranking method.

There is a single path to the top event for each basic event. The importance of the event e_1 will be given by all the weights of the gates that are in the path from this event to the top event. For example, the importance for the events 1 and 2 (Fig. 3.21) will be:

$$I_{e_1} = 0.75 \cdot 0.25 \cdot 0.75 = 0.140625$$

$$I_{e_2} = 0.125 \cdot 0.75 \cdot 0.25 \cdot 0.75 = 0 \cdot 017578$$

The importance measures of the basic events employing the new approach are given in Table 3.2, being the ranking: $e_8 < e_5 < e_6 < e_7 < e_1 < e_9 < e_{10} < e_2 < e_3 < e_4$, obtaining 20 cut-sets, where 22 cut-sets are obtained by employing the AND criterion with the ranking $e_8 < e_1 < e_5 < e_6 < e_7 < e_9 < e_{10} < e_2 < e_3 < e_4$. The main reason that the new approach provides better results than the AND criterion is because of the importance of e_1 the same to $e_5, e_6,$ and e_7 according to the AND criterion, i.e., e_1 is more important due to its location in the FT.

Table 3.2 Importance of basic events

Basic event	e_1	e_2	e_3	e_4	e_5	e_6	e_7	e_8	e_9	e_{10}
Importance	0.1406	0.0176	0.0176	0.0176	0.1641	0.1641	0.1641	0.1875	0.1406	0.1406

The new method considers that $e_5, e_6,$ and e_7 are connected by an OR logic gate, which means that the failure is more probable to happen through it, i.e., $e_5, e_6,$ and e_7 are given more importance than e_1.

3.3.4 Case Study

A set of LDTs have been considered for evaluating the ranking events. The number of basic events, intermediate events, OR, and AND gates and levels are defined for each LDT in the following Table 3.3.

Table 3.3 LDTs characteristics

	Number of basic events	Number of intermediate events	Number of OR gates	Number of AND gates	Number of levels
LDT 1	5	5	3	3	3
LDT 2	15	13	10	4	8
LDT 3	11	9	5	5	6
LDT 4	25	21	16	6	12
LDT 5	20	15	10	6	5
LDT 6	12	7	5	3	4
LDT 7	10	7	7	1	5
LDT 8	20	17	12	6	11
LDT 9	31	25	16	10	11

The aforementioned methods have been employed for ranking the events of the LDTs shown in Table 3.3. The number of cut-sets obtained by using each method is given in Table 3.4.

Table 3.4 Cut-sets obtained by the ranking events

	TDLR	DFS	BFS	Level	AND	Approach
LDT 1	2	2	2	2	2	2
LDT 2	30	30	155	30	30	30
LDT 3	12	24	36	12	12	12
LDT 4	64	142	176	64	22	28
LDT 5	99	207	257	99	55	55
LDT 6	9	7	7	9	9	12
LDT 7	9	12	21	9	9	9
LDT 8	44	76	192	44	44	44
LDT 9	1012	1292	3456	1012	1012	924

BFS provides poor results in most of the cases, especially when the LDT has a large number of events, levels, and "or" and "and" gates. The Level and AND methods generate the ranking of the events with a minimal cut-sets. The conclusions relating to Level, DFS, and TDLR methods should be studied for each LDT.

The new approach proposed in this book provides the minimal cut-sets in most of the cases, i.e., for FT 1–3, 5, 7–9, being the number of cut-sets close to the minimal cut-sets found for LDT 4 and 6. The new approach could improve the minimal cut-sets for LDT 9, the most complex LDT taken into account.

There is not a specific heuristic method appropriate for all the LDTs. Some methods are more appropriate than others depending on the logical function, i.e., the most appropriate method should be chosen for each case. The heuristic methods described hereby are static. There are also dynamic heuristic methods, however, they are not suitable for large or complex LDTs. They present some drawbacks such as they need to store in memory the BDD or a part of it.[67]

3.4 EVALUATION OF BINARY DECISION DIAGRAMS

The information that can be obtained from a BDD following the steps in Fig. 3.22 is:

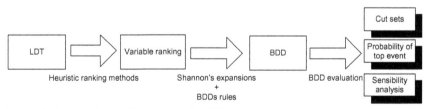

Fig. 3.22 Stages of the LDT analysis via BDD.

- MCSs and Minimal Path Sets.
- Probability of occurrence of the top event.
- Sensitivity analysis and importance measures.

3.4.1 Cut Sets and Critical Paths

The CSs of a BDD are the paths from the root node to the terminal nodes with value 1, abovementioned. Once the set of paths of the BDD have been obtained, simplification rules (idempotent and absorption) of Boolean algebra will be applied to eliminate redundant groups. The groups obtained after the simplifications are called MCSs.

If an optimal variable ranking has been chosen, then the resulting BDD will have a minimum size and the paths to the terminal nodes with value 1 will be the *MCSs*. Simplification rules should be applied to achieve the MCSs if an inappropriate ranking has been chosen. An example is shown in Fig. 3.23.

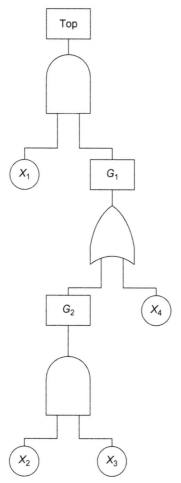

Fig. 3.23 LDT for $f = x_1 x_2 x_3 + x_1 x_4$.

The logical function of the system corresponds to the following expression:

$$f(x_1, x_2, x_3, x_4) = x_1(x_2, x_3 + x_4) = x_1 x_2 x_3 + x_1 x_4$$

Applying the Shannon's expansion according to Eq. (3.1), with the ranking $x_1 < x_2 < x_3 < x_4$, the following expression is obtained:

$$f = ite(x_1, ite(x_2, ite(x_3, 1, x_4), x_4), 0)$$

This logical function can be represented with the BDD given in Fig. 3.24.

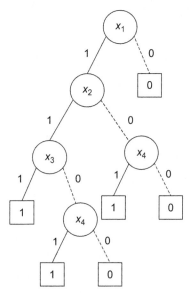

Fig. 3.24 BDD for $f = x_1 \ x_2 \ x_3 + x_1 \ x_4$.

The following CSs are obtained following the paths to the terminal vertices with value 1:

$$CS1 = x_1 x_2 x_3$$

$$CS2 = x_1 x_4$$

$$CS3 = x_1 x_2 x_4$$

The variable ranking is not optimal in this case and the MCSs have not been obtained directly. Applying absorption rules, the resulting MCSs are:

$CS1 = MCS1 = x_1 x_2 x_3$

$CS2 = MCS2 = x_1 x_4$

3.4.2 Probability of the Top Event

The main advantage of the quantitative analysis via BDD is that the probability of occurrence of the top event can be exactly achieved.

The paths of a BDD are independent. The probability of the top event is the sum of the probabilities of the CSs. For a BDD with a total of Np paths, the probability of occurrence of the top event is:

$$Q_{sys} = \sum_{i=1}^{N_p} P(CS_i) \tag{3.19}$$

The probability of a CS is the product of the probabilities of the events that appear in the CS. Therefore, the probability of the top event in Fig. 3.21 is:

$$Q_{sys} = q_1 q_2 q_3 + q_1 q_2 (1 - q_3) q_4 + q_1 (1 - q_2) q_4$$

where it can be simplified as:

$$Q_{sys} = q_1 q_2 q_3 + q_1 q_4 - q_1 q_2 q_3 q_4$$

The main advantage of a quantitative analysis using BDDs is the implicit formulation. Coudert (1994) proposed the use of the name "metaproducts" to develop implicit calculations of the BDDs.[73]

3.4.3 Sensitivity Analysis and Importance Measures

The IMs defined in Chapter 2 can be calculated from the BDDs. *Rauzy* (1993) defines efficient algorithms based on BDDs to calculate IMs that provide exact results.[68]

3.5 ADVANTAGES OF THE BINARY DECISION DIAGRAMS

BDDs present the following advantages:
- The computational cost is independent of the number of PIs and the way in which the LDT is built.
- All the PIs are taken into account.
- PIs provide exact qualitative and quantitative information.
- The computational speed is between 100 and 1000 times higher than using classic methods.
- Typical operators of Boolean algebra can be evaluated with quadratic complexity.
- The cost of the analysis using BDD depends on the LDT size.

- Large Boolean functions can be represented with relatively small diagrams.
- Operations with "Products" over the time are linear with respect to the BDD size.
- Great efficiency in the treatment of noncoherent LDTs.

Table 3.5 shows a comparison between the main characteristics of the LDTs and BDDs, besides the aforementioned characteristics of the LDTs.

Table 3.5 Benefits and drawbacks

LDT	BDD
Right depiction of a DM problem	Poor depiction of a DM problem
Mathematical issues when trying to find the solution	Great efficiency finding the solution[a]
Poor software implementation	Well-grounded background to achieve mathematical solutions
Lack of reliable software to treat this kind of problems	Accurate software and low computational time[a]
No qualification needed by employees to depict a DM problem	Great complex associated and software is essential to obtain it

[a]The advantages of using BDDs, i.e, the good points provided by BDDs.

The conversion process from LDT to BDD allows for obtaining a right depiction of the DM problem and an accurate solution.

CHAPTER 4

Case Studies

4.1 LDT WITHOUT MOEs

A logical decision tree (LDT) with three levels and without MOEs is presented in Fig. 4.1.

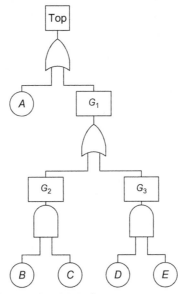

Fig. 4.1 Simple LDT without MOEs (LDT01).

Firstly, an event ranking must be set. The LDT is very simple, therefore it can be seen that the event A must be located in first place. The rest of the events can be placed in random order because of the symmetry of the LDT. The next ranking is obtained using the *TDLR* method: $A < B < C < D < E$

$$G_2 = ite(B, 1, 0) \cdot ite(C, 1, 0) = ite(B, ite(C, 1, 0), 0)$$

$$G_3 = ite(D, 1, 0) \cdot ite(E, 1, 0) = ite(D, ite(E, 1, 0), 0)$$

Decision-Making Management
http://dx.doi.org/10.1016/B978-0-12-811540-4.00004-1

53

$$G_1 = ite(B, ite(C, 1, 0), 0) + ite(D, ite(E, 1, 0), 0)$$
$$= ite(B, ite(C, 1, 0) + ite(D, ite(E, 1, 0), 0), ite(D, ite(E, 1, 0), 0))$$
$$= ite(B, ite(C, 1, ite(D, ite(E, 1, 0), 0)), ite(D, ite(E, 1, 0), 0))$$
$$Top = ite(A, 1, 0) + ite(B, ite(C, 1, ite(D, ite(E, 1, 0), 0)),$$
$$ite(D, ite(E, 1, 0), 0))$$
$$= ite(A, 1, ite(B, ite(B, ite(C, 1, ite(D, ite(E, 1, 0), 0)),$$
$$ite(D, ite(E, 1, 0), 0))))$$

The equivalent binary decision diagrams (BDD) is shown in Fig. 4.2.

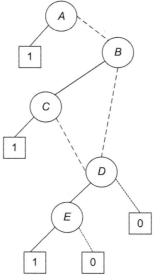

Fig. 4.2 *BDD* corresponding to LDT01.

The probability of the top event obtained by the sum of the probabilities of each CS is given by:

$$Q_{sys} = q_A + (1 - q_A)q_B q_C + (1 - q_A)q_B(1 - q_C)q_D q_E$$
$$+ (1 - q_A)(1 - q_B)q_D q_E$$

4.2 LDT WITH A MOE AT THE SAME LEVEL

The LDT presented in Fig. 4.3 considers that one event has been replaced from the LDT given in Fig. 4.2 to generate a MOE.

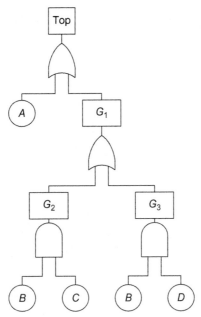

Fig. 4.3 LDT with a MOE (LDT02).

The MOE B must be more important than the events C and D. There-fore, the ranking is: $A < B < C < D$, being the BDD shown in Fig. 4.4:

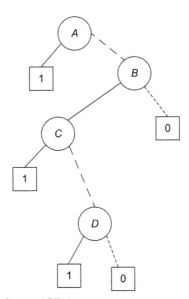

Fig. 4.4 *BDD* corresponding to LDT02.

The probability of occurrence of the top event is:

$$Q_{sys} = q_A + (1 - q_A)q_B q_C + (1 - q_A)q_B(1 - q_C)q_D$$

4.3 LDT WITH MOEs AT DIFFERENT LEVELS

The event B is repeated at two different levels, see Fig. 4.5.

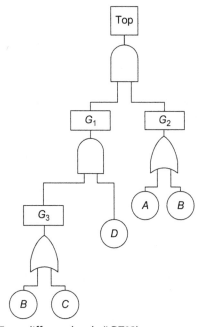

Fig. 4.5 LDT with MOEs at different levels (LDT03).

In this case there are different solutions depending on the heuristic method employed. The best ranking is:

$$B < A < C < D$$

Applying the operation rules of BDDs, then:

$$G_3 = ite(B, 1, ite(C, 1, 0))$$
$$G_2 = ite(B, 1, ite(A, 1, 0))$$
$$G_1 = ite(B, 1, ite(C, 1, 0)) \cdot ite(D, 1, 0)$$
$$= ite(B, 1 \cdot ite(D, 1, 0), ite(C, 1, 0) \cdot ite(D, 1, 0))$$
$$= ite(B, ite(D, 1, 0), ite(C, D, 0))$$

$$Top = ite(B, ite(D, 1, 0), ite(C, D, 0)) \cdot ite(B, 1, ite(A, 1, 0))$$
$$= ite(B, ite(D, 1, 0), ite(A, 1, 0) \cdot ite(C, D, 0))$$
$$= ite(B, ite(D, 1, 0), ite(A, ite(C, D, 0), 0))$$

The reduced BDD is shown in Fig. 4.6.

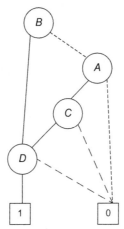

Fig. 4.6 BDD corresponding to LDT03.

In this case, there are only two CSs. The probability of occurrence of the top event is:

$$Q_{sys} = q_B q_D + (1 - q_B) q_A q_C q_D$$

4.4 LDT ALTERNATING AND AND OR GATES AT DIFFERENT LEVELS

Fig. 4.7 shows a LDT where OR and AND gates are alternated.

Being the ranking as: $A < B < C < D < E$. Applying the operation rules of BDDs:

$$Top = ite(A, 1, ite(B, ite(C, 1, ite(D, ite(E, 1, 0), 0)), 0))$$

The BDD is presented in Fig. 4.8.

There are three CSs, being the probability of occurrence of the top event:

$$Q_{sys} = q_A + (1 - q_A) q_B q_C + (1 - q_A) q_B (1 - q_C) q_D q_E$$

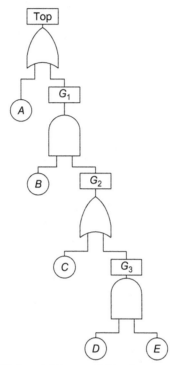

Fig. 4.7 LDT alternating AND and OR gates (LDT04).

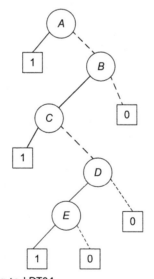

Fig. 4.8 BDD corresponding to LDT04.

4.5 LDT WITH SEVERAL MOEs AT DIFFERENT LEVELS

Fig. 4.9 presents a LDT with several MOEs. The variable ranking for this LDT is not direct. Different ranking methods will be applied to establish an appropriate ranking.

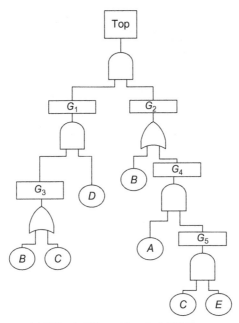

Fig. 4.9 LDT with several MOEs at different levels (LDT05).

- Weights method

The weights are assigned to each gate:

$$W(G_5) = W(C) + W(E) = 1 + 1 = 2$$
$$W(G_4) = W(A) + W(G_5) = 1 + 2 = 3$$
$$W(G_3) = W(B) + W(C) = 1 + 1 = 2$$
$$W(G_2) = W(B) + W(G_4) = 1 + 3 = 4$$
$$W(G_1) = W(G_3) + W(D) = 2 + 1 = 3$$

The logical expressions are rewritten in the output of each gate G_j because the inputs appear in order of increasing weights:

$$G_5 = C + E$$
$$G_4 = A + G_5$$
$$G_3 = B + C$$
$$G_2 = B + G_4$$
$$G_1 = D + G_3$$

The LDT is reordered. It is observed that the expression G_1 has changed. A DSF exploration is performed according to this new variable ranking. Table 4.1 shows the rankings obtained for different ranking methods.

Table 4.1 Comparison of different heuristic methods for LDT05

Events	DFS	Top-down, left-right	Level	Weights	Structural	AND method AND gates	(Rank)
A	(4)	(4)	3	(4)	3/64 (4)	2	(3)
B	(1)	(2)	3,2	(2)	30/64 (1)	2,1	(1)
C	(2)	(3)	3,4	(3)	12/64 (3)	2,3	(5)
D	(3)	(1)	2	(1)	27/64 (2)	2	(2)
E	(5)	(5)	4	(5)	3/64 (5)	3	(4)

Different results are obtained for each ranking method. The following order is obtained using the weights and the TDLR methods: $D < B < C < A < E$. The BDD obtained with this ranking is given in Fig. 4.10

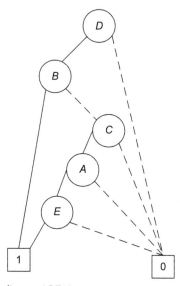

Fig. 4.10 BDD corresponding to LDT05.

The probability of occurrence of the Top Event will be:

$$Q_{sys} = q_D q_B + q_D(1 - q_B)q_C q_A q_E$$

4.6 NEW APPROACH TO REDUCE COMPUTATIONAL COST

The DM problem described is a NP-hard type and, therefore, for a large number of BCs, or a complex topology, the computational cost is significant. This section presents a novel approach for finding a solution close to the optimal result to minimize the computational cost. This approach is based on the logical gates, especially the AND gates, the number and the position on the tree (level), and their effects on the solution and the computational cost of the system. The reference solutions, or experimental solutions, are obtained in simple systems, then, they are extrapolated to complex systems via polynomial regressive functions.

The LDT in Fig. 4.11 has been evaluated for the cases marked in black in Fig. 4.12, and the values marked in red are the estimated results. The AND criterion has been employed for ranking the BCs.

The estimations are calculated employing polynomial expressions, where the polynomial degree depends on the number of experimental points obtained. The results have been obtained using the algorithms developed by Artigao.[74]

Fig. 4.13 shows the results of probabilities found exactly (E) by BDD and the predicted (P) results found by the new approach. It is observed that the probability is indirectly proportional to the number of AND gates, and proportional to the level, which is expected. Moreover, the consequences of adding a new AND gate is indirectly proportional to the level. In Fig. 4.13 is also plotted (black curve) the absolute deviation expressed as abs($(E-P)/P$). The deviation is proportional to the number of gates, with values always inferior to 0.45%. It demonstrates that the accuracy of the solutions founds by the new approach is high in every case.

The deviation has been estimated for different levels and number of AND gates by quadratic polynomial expression. It is useful to know approximately the probability accuracy estimated, shown in Fig. 4.14.

A similar study presented in Fig. 4.13 has been done taking into account the number of CSs, see Fig. 4.15. The number of CSs is larger in each level when the number of AND gates increase, and the number of CSs is smaller when the level is larger taking into account the same number of AND gates. The error is less relevant for CSs than for the probabilities, because of the same independently of the number of CSs. It is relevant to estimate the computational cost for solving the problem that is proportional to the CSs size. Exponential expressions have been used to evaluate the CSs size.

Probability of occurrence of MP						Number of AND gates	Number of cut-sets					
Level 1	Level 2	Level 3	Level 4	Level 5	Level 6		Level 6	Level 5	Level 4	Level 3	Level 2	Level 1
0.0756	0.291	0.3864	0.4313	0.4531	0.4638	1	63	64	72	112	288	1024
	0.0436	0.2836	0.3846	0.4308	0.453	2	63	72	144	672	4608	
		0.1637	0.3341	0.4077	0.4419	3	65	104	536	5840		
		0.027	0.2795	0.3837	0.4306	4	71	208	2528	15,616		
			0.2205	0.3587	0.4191	5	85	528	7400			
			0.1578	0.3326	0.4074	6	115	1496	16,432			
			0.0911	0.3036	0.3954	7	177	3673	30,904			
			0.0204	0.2752	0.3832	8	303	7836	52,095			
				0.2458	0.3727	9	527	14,952				
				0.2154	0.3604	10	896	26,177				
				0.184	0.3479	11	1463	42,860				
				0.1516	0.3352	12	2294	66,544				
				0.1182	0.3223	13	3462	98,961				
				0.0838	0.3092	14	5048	142,036				
				0.0484	0.2959	15	7144	197,888				
				0.012	0.2824	16	9850	268,825				
					0.2687	17	13,276					
					0.2548	18	17,540					
					0.2407	19	22,770					
					0.2264	20	29,103					
					0.2119	21	36,684					
					0.1972	22	45,669					
					0.1823	23	56,221					
					0.1672	24	68,513					
					0.1519	25	82,729					
					0.1364	26	99,058					
					0.1207	27	117,701					
					0.1048	28	138,869					
					0.0887	29	162,778					
					0.0724	30	189,658					
					0.0559	31	219,744					
					0.0392	32	253,283					

Fig. 4.11 LDT case considered for topologic study.

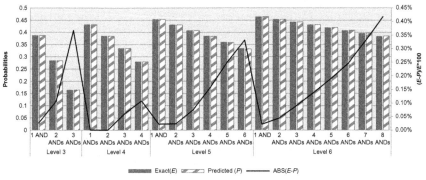

Fig. 4.12 Experimental results and estimations.

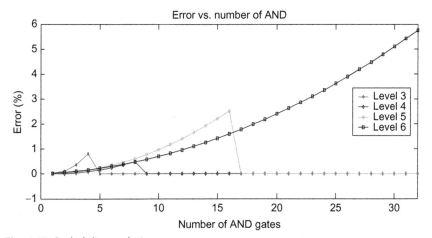

Fig. 4.13 Probability analysis.

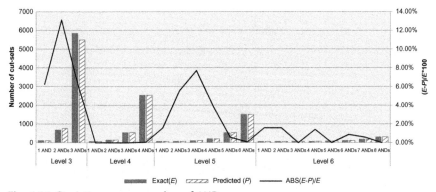

Fig. 4.14 Deviation versus number of AND.

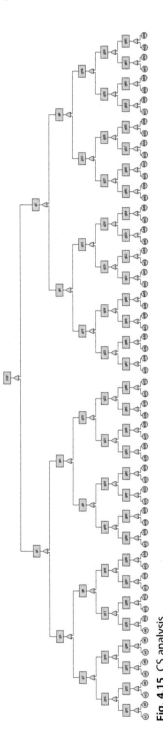

Fig. 4.15 CS analysis.

CHAPTER 5

Dynamic Analysis of LDT

5.1 INTRODUCTION

The conversion from logical decision tree (LDT) to binary decision diagrams (BDD) is mainly due to the analytical expression provided by the BDD. It allows reducing the computational cost when an analysis over the time is required because it is not necessary to solve the LDT at every iteration. This chapter explains how to employ this expression to collect the occurrence probability of a top event over the time. It is important to remark that this book focuses on the study of static LDT and not dynamic ones, i.e., the topology of the tree remains immutable at any period.

The LDT considered in this section is composed of nine BCs (Fig. 5.1). There is a large number of alternatives for a direct LDTA when the LTD is bigger and composed of hundreds or thousands of BCs. The BDD shown in Fig. 5.2 is obtained from the LDT given in Fig. 5.1.

The paths starting from the top BC to a terminal 1 vertex provide a certain state in that MP will occur, i.e., cut-sets. The BDD shown in Fig. 5.2 has the following 14 cut-sets:

$CS1 : BC7$

$CS2 : \overline{BC7} \cdot BC1 \cdot BC3$

$CS3 : \overline{BC7} \cdot BC1 \cdot \overline{BC3} \cdot BC4$

$CS4 : \overline{BC7} \cdot BC1 \cdot \overline{BC3} \cdot \overline{BC4} \cdot BC8 \cdot BC9$

$CS5 : \overline{BC7} \cdot BC1 \cdot \overline{BC3} \cdot \overline{BC4} \cdot BC8 \cdot \overline{BC9} \cdot BC5 \cdot BC6$

$CS6 : \overline{BC7} \cdot BC1 \cdot \overline{BC3} \cdot \overline{BC4} \cdot \overline{BC8} \cdot BC5 \cdot BC6$

$CS7 : \overline{BC7} \cdot \overline{BC1} \cdot BC2 \cdot BC3$

$CS8 : \overline{BC7} \cdot \overline{BC1} \cdot BC2 \cdot \overline{BC3} \cdot BC4$

$CS9 : \overline{BC7} \cdot \overline{BC1} \cdot BC2 \cdot \overline{BC3} \cdot \overline{BC4} \cdot BC8 \cdot BC9$

$CS10 : \overline{BC7} \cdot \overline{BC1} \cdot BC2 \cdot \overline{BC3} \cdot \overline{BC4} \cdot BC8 \cdot \overline{BC9} \cdot BC5 \cdot BC6$

$CS11 : \overline{BC7} \cdot \overline{BC1} \cdot BC2 \cdot \overline{BC3} \cdot \overline{BC4} \cdot \overline{BC8} \cdot BC5 \cdot BC6$

Decision-Making Management
http://dx.doi.org/10.1016/B978-0-12-811540-4.00005-3

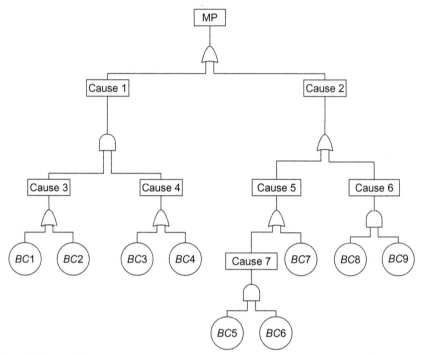

Fig. 5.1 Logical decision tree.

$$CS12 : \overline{BC7} \cdot \overline{BC1} \cdot \overline{BC2} \cdot BC8 \cdot BC9$$

$$CS13 : \overline{BC7} \cdot \overline{BC1} \cdot \overline{BC2} \cdot BC8 \cdot \overline{BC9} \cdot BC5 \cdot BC6$$

$$CS14 : \overline{BC7} \cdot \overline{BC1} \cdot \overline{BC2} \cdot \overline{BC8} \cdot BC5 \cdot BC6 \qquad (5.1)$$

The probability of occurrence must be assigned to each BC, being $P(BCi)$ the probability of occurrence of the ith BC. $P\left(\overline{BCi}\right)$ is the probability of nonoccurrence of the ith BC. Therefore:

$$P\left(\overline{BCi}\right) = 1 - P(BCi) \qquad (5.2)$$

The occurrence probability of the jth cut-set ($P(CSj)$) can be calculated as the product of the probabilities of the BCs that compose the cut-set, i.e., $P(BCi)$ and $P\left(\overline{BCi}\right)$. For example, the probability of the CS3 is:

$$P(CS3) = (1 - P(BC7)) \cdot P(BC1) \cdot (1 - P(BC3)) \cdot P(BC4) \qquad (5.3)$$

The probability of MP (Q_{MP}) can be obtained by Eq. (5.4).

$$Q_{MP} = \sum_{j=1}^{n} P(CSj) \qquad (5.4)$$

where n is the total number of cut-sets.

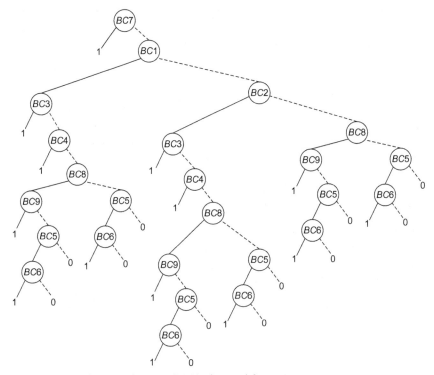

Fig. 5.2 Binary decision diagram (BDD) obtained from Fig. 5.1.

5.2 CASE STUDY 1

5.2.1 Probability Functions

The probability of the BCs is calculated by attending to the following time-dependant functions.[75,76] These functions have been considered for different behaviors of the BCs.

5.2.1.1 Constant Probability
In this case the probability of the BC is constant.

$$Q_{MP}(t) = K \tag{5.5}$$

being K a constant value between 0 and 1.

5.2.1.2 Exponential Increasing Probability
The probability function assigned is:

$$Q_{MP}(t) = 1 - e^{-\lambda t} \tag{5.6}$$

where λ is a parameter that takes only positive values and determines how fast the probability rises.

5.2.1.3 Linear Decreasing Probability

The probability function is:

$$Q_{MP}(t) = 1 - mt \tag{5.7}$$

where m determines how quickly the probability decreases.

5.2.1.4 Periodic Probability

In this model, BCs have a periodic behavior, where the expression is given by:

$$Q_{MP}(t) = 1 - e^{-\lambda(t-n\alpha)}, \quad n = 1, 2, 3, \ldots \tag{5.8}$$

where $-\lambda > 0$ and α determines the size of the period.

The probability assignment for BCs in Fig. 5.1 has been done to obtain $Q_{MP}(t)$, see Table 5.1.

Table 5.1 Probability functions

Basic causes	Probability model	Parameters
BC1	Constant	$K = 0.5$
BC2	Exponential increasing	$\lambda = 0.5$
BC3	Linear decreasing	$m = 1/8$
BC4	Periodic	$\lambda = 0.1, \alpha = 1$
BC5	Constant	$K = 0.4$
BC6	Exponential increasing	$\lambda = 0.2$
BC7	Constant	$K = 0.3$
BC8	Constant	$K = 0.7$
BC9	Linear decreasing	$m = 1/10$

Fig. 5.3 shows $Q_{MP}(t)$ obtained with 600 samples.

Investments at different times will produce different results according to Fig. 5.3, i.e., if resources are invested at wrong time it could lead to ineffective outcomes.

5.2.2 Importance Measure Analysis

IMs are employed to classify the most important BCs of the LDT. The main methods for measuring the importance of BCs have been described, e.g., Fussell-Vesely, Birnbaum, and Criticality. In this case study, the *Fussell-Vesely* importance measure has been chosen to analyze the importance of BCs. This IM was defined as the quotient between the probability of CSs that contain a BC and Q_{MP}.

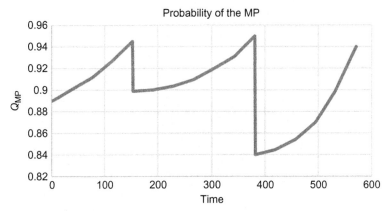

Fig. 5.3 Probability of MP occurrence.

$$I_k^{FV}(t) = \frac{P\left(CS_1 \cup CS_2 \cup CS_3 \ldots \cup CS_j\right)}{Q_{MP}}$$

where $-I_k^{FV}(t)$ is the Fussell-Vesely IM value of k BC at time t. $-P\left(CS_1(t) \cup CS_2(t) \cup CS_3(t) \ldots \cup CS_j(t)\right)$ is the probability of the union of the CSs that contains the k BC.

If a certain BC exists in many CSs, it could be considered very important. It is a significant problem because irrelevant BCs can have higher I_k^{FV} than the really important BCs.

Fussell-Vesely IM has been calculated for each BC on 600 units of time. IMs of BCs vary over the time, see Fig. 5.4. Therefore, different importance rankings could be done. For example, if an investment is done at $t=8$, then the resources should be done to the BCs according to the following priority:

$$BC_3 > BC_1 > BC_7 > BC_8 > BC_9 > BC_2 > BC_5 > BC_6 > BC_4$$

However, if the investment is made at $t=500$, then the resources should be assigned in the following order:

$$BC_7 > BC_1 > BC_2 > BC_3 > BC_4 > BC_8 > BC_9 > BC_5 > BC_6$$

5.3 CASE STUDY 2

5.3.1 Probability Set

Fig. 5.5 shows a LDT,[77] being the main objective to minimize the probability of occurrence of the Top Event.

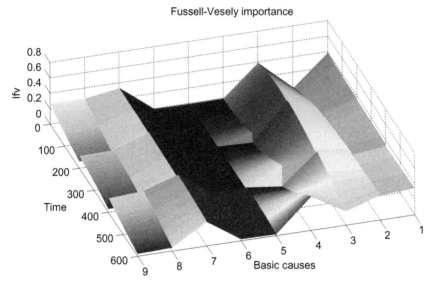

Fig. 5.4 Fussel-Vesely IMs.

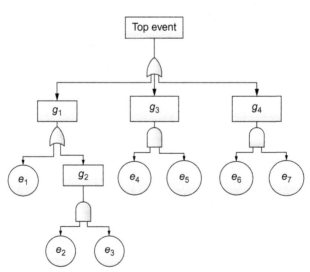

Fig. 5.5 LDT dynamic analysis example.

The resultant BDD is achieved from the LDT to BDD conversion software.[74] Thus, the associated CSs are:

$$CS_1 = e_1$$
$$CS_2 = e_6 \cdot \overline{e_1}$$
$$CS_3 = e_7 \cdot \overline{e_6} \cdot \overline{e_1}$$
$$CS_4 = e_5 \cdot e_4 \cdot \overline{e_7} \cdot \overline{e_6} \cdot \overline{e_1}$$
$$CS_5 = e_3 \cdot e_2 \cdot \overline{e_5} \cdot e_4 \cdot \overline{e_7} \cdot \overline{e_6} \cdot \overline{e_1}$$
$$CS_6 = e_3 \cdot e_2 \cdot \overline{e_4} \cdot \overline{e_7} \cdot \overline{e_6} \cdot \overline{e_1}$$

The analytical expression for the LDT for dynamic analysis is:

$$
\begin{aligned}
Q_{MP}(t) = \ & q_1(t) + q_6(t) \cdot (1 - q_1(t)) + q_7(t) \cdot (1 - q_6(t)) \cdot (1 - q_1(t)) \\
& + q_5 \cdot q_4 \cdot (1 - q_7) \cdot (1 - q_6) \cdot (1 - q_1) \\
& + q_3 \cdot q_2 \cdot (1 - q_5) \cdot (1 - q_7) \cdot (1 - q_6) \cdot (1 - q_1) \\
& + q_3 \cdot q_2 \cdot (1 - q_4)(1 - q_7) \cdot (1 - q_6) \cdot (1 - q_1)
\end{aligned}
$$

As aforementioned, the static LDTs are those whose topology does not change over the time, however, it is considered that the probability of the basic events can vary over the time. The probability of the events can be obtained from statistical studies, where certain mathematical models adapt the behavior of the event over the time to a certain analytical model.[78–81] The same time-dependent functions considered in Section 5.2.1 have been taken into account in this section for representing events with different behavior over the time.

Fig. 5.6 shows an example of the models. These models can be modified or combined to adapt them to a certain event. Fig. 5.1 has been created using the following data:

Constant probability $\rightarrow q_i(t) = 0.3$
Exponential increasing probability $\rightarrow q_i(t) = 1 - e^{-2t}, \quad \lambda > 0$
Linear increasing probability $\rightarrow q_i(t) = 0.06t$
Periodic probability $\rightarrow q_i(t) = 1 - e^{-0.4(t-n2)}$

This set of probability data can be used as a variable input for the probability function obtained by the BDD.

The dynamic analysis is based on developing an iterative process considering the analytical behavior of the events. The occurrence probability of the i event at time t is defined as q_i^t. These probabilities are collected in a n x m matrix ($PV(i,t)$), where n is the number of events and m number of iterations. PV is defined as follows:

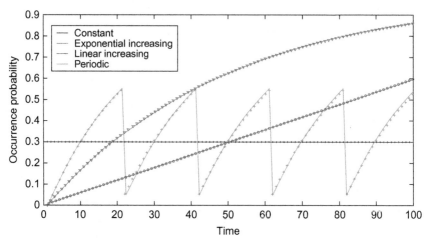

Fig. 5.6 Dynamic occurrence probabilities.

$$\mathbf{PV}(i, t) = \begin{bmatrix} q_1^1 & q_1^2 & \cdots & q_1^{m-1} & q_1^m \\ q_2^1 & q_2^2 & & q_2^{m-1} & q_2^m \\ \vdots & & \ddots & & \vdots \\ q_{n-1}^1 & q_{n-1}^2 & \cdots & q_{n-1}^{m-1} & q_{n-1}^m \\ q_n^1 & q_n^2 & & q_n^{m-1} & q_n^m \end{bmatrix}$$

where each component q_i^t corresponds to the occurrence probability of the event i at time t. Fig. 5.7 shows the flowchart for obtaining **PV** in order to save the probabilities automatically.

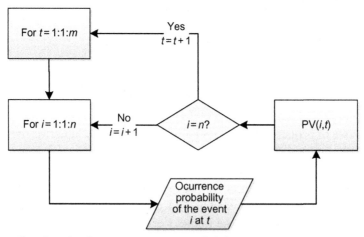

Fig. 5.7 Flowchart for dynamic occurrence probabilities.

It is possible to use this matrix as an input in the iterative process when the $PV(i,t)$ is obtained. The main advantage of using BDDs for the dynamic analysis is that LDT has to be solved only once to extract its probability function. The iterative process is based on the evaluation of this probability function using the corresponding probabilities provided by PV at each iteration.

For example, the data shown in Fig. 5.6 is collected by the following PV matrix for the first five iterations:

$$PV(i, t) = \begin{bmatrix} 0.00 & 0.04 & 0.08 & 0.11 & 0.15 & 0.18 \\ 0.30 & 0.30 & 0.30 & 0.30 & 0.30 & 0.30 \\ 0.00 & 0.18 & 0.33 & 0.45 & 0.55 & 0.63 \\ 0.00 & 0.06 & 0.02 & 0.02 & 0.02 & 0.03 \end{bmatrix}$$

Therefore, the probability vector corresponds to a different column of the PV matrix at each iteration.

5.3.2 Dynamic Analysis Example

The probability assignments are based on the parameters collected in Table 5.2.

Table 5.2 Probability assignment example

	Mathematical model	Parameters
Event 1	Constant	$q=0.3$
Event 2	Linear increasing	$m=0.06$
Event 3	Exponential increasing	$\lambda=2$
Event 4	Periodic	$\lambda=0.4,$ $\alpha=2$
Event 5	Constant	$q=0.2$
Event 6	Periodic	$\lambda=0.6,$ $\alpha=3$
Event 7	Exponential increasing	$\lambda=3$

Fig. 5.8 shows the probabilities of the events over 100 samples. Each sample may represent a certain increment of time.

The probability of the top event Q_{Sys} over the time is set considering the probability assignment. Fig. 5.9 shows this probability, with a general rising trend. The function is not always rising because there are events with periodic probability functions. This probability has been obtained for 50 samples. The curve presented in Fig. 5.9 can be employed to do prognostics, to fit the operations thresholds, etc.

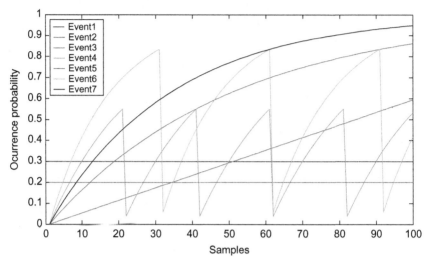

Fig. 5.8 Probability assignment. Example.

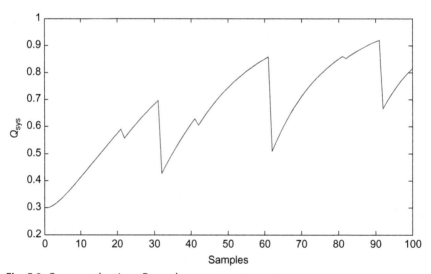

Fig. 5.9 Q_{MP} over the time. Example.

The dynamic analysis proposed in this book can facilitate establishing a maintenance planning because the probability of the top event is available over the time. It leads to keep the reliability of this event under control.

5.3.3 Dynamic Importance Measure

The procedure mentioned in previous section is used to carry out a dynamic IM analysis. The IM is calculated for all the events and iterations. This information is very useful to establish a variable ranking over the time and, consequently, to determine the most significant events in a certain period.

Fig. 5.10 shows the Birnbaum importance calculated for 100 samples. The importance is variable over the time and the ranking of the most critical events also varies, e.g., the event e_1 is the most important event at the first sample, however, event e_7 is the most important at the sample 60th, i.e., the period function of different events should be taken into account to optimize the resource allocation.

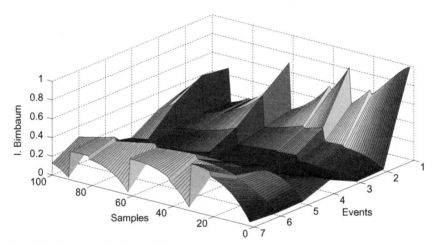

Fig. 5.10 Dynamic Birnbaum IM. Example.

Fig. 5.11 shows the Criticality IM calculated for 100 samples. It considers the occurrence probabilities of the events. It generates different results with regard to the Birnbaum IM.

Fig. 5.12 shows the Fussel-Vesely IM for 100 samples.

In general, the results are similar in the three cases. Each measure has a different meaning and, therefore, one of them should be selected according to the objectives of the DM process.

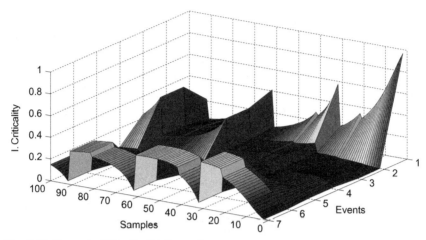

Fig. 5.11 Dynamic Criticality IM. Example.

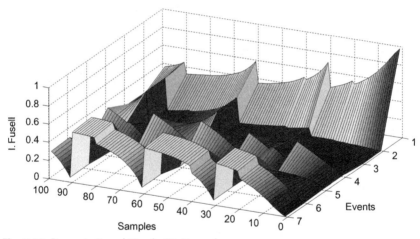

Fig. 5.12 Dynamic Fussel-Vesely IM. Example.

CHAPTER 6

DM Optimization

6.1 INTRODUCTION

The conversion from logical decision tree (LDT) to binary decision diagram (BDD) was presented in Chapters 3 and 4. This method allows for obtaining the analytical expression of the top event occurrence probability in function of the probabilities of basic events. This expression defines quantitatively the behavior of a system, or process, but it does not take into account the exogenous variables that, in certain cases, could be more influential than the endogenous ones.

This chapter presents a novel approach to consider external factors that may be important for optimizing the DM processes.[82] It is based on considering the analytical expression obtained from the BDD as the objective function of a NLPP, where the exogenous variables are modeled by a set of constraints.[83]

An optimal investment, subject to the limitation of resources, is the main objective of the DM process. This book proposes two strategies to support the resource allocation when a MP is given. Fig. 6.1 shows the steps to be done before using the novel methods.

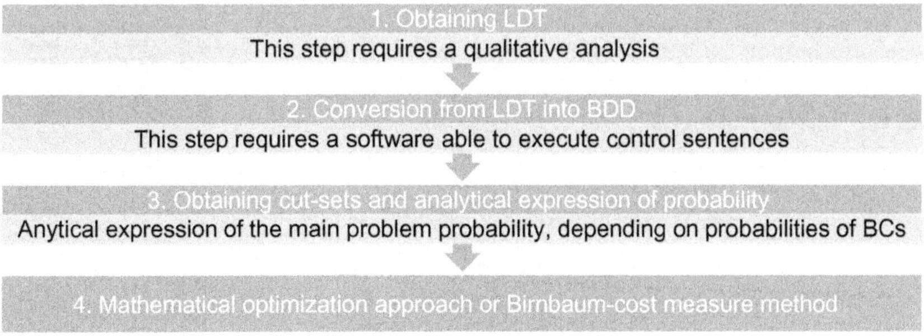

1. Obtaining LDT
This step requires a qualitative analysis

2. Conversion from LDT into BDD
This step requires a software able to execute control sentences

3. Obtaining cut-sets and analytical expression of probability
Anytical expression of the main problem probability, depending on probabilities of BCs

4. Mathematical optimization approach or Birnbaum-cost measure method

Fig. 6.1 Proposed optimization method process.

Decision-Making Management
http://dx.doi.org/10.1016/B978-0-12-811540-4.00006-5

6.2 DM APPROACH

The LDT design is not complicated, but it requires an adequate knowledge of the problem. Fig. 6.2 is composed of 32 basic causes and 26 nonbasic causes. One of the branches of this LDT has been zoomed in Fig. 6.2 to show some causes in detail. The MP is "delay in the orders," therefore, the business is seeking to minimize these delays.

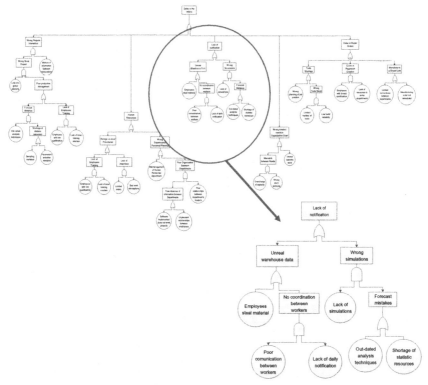

Fig. 6.2 Example of a LDT.

The following procedure is suggested to create a LDT:
- Define properly the MP and its scope.
- Detect the BCs related with the MP.
- Study the interrelation between mentioned BCs and the MP.
- Obtain the probability data for each BC.[84]

6.3 Mathematical NLPP Background

The problem to address in this section is:

$$minimize\ f(x)$$

$$subject\ to\ \ h(x) = 0$$

$$g(x) \leq 0$$

where in case that any of the functions involved are nonlinear, the problem will be a Non-Linear Programming Problem (NLPP).[85] NLPP is defined by a function $f : R^n \to R$, and two vector functions that represent the constraints.

$$h : R^n \to R^m$$

$$g : R^n \to R^d$$

$$x \in R^n$$

$$f : R^n \to R$$

being m the number of (nonlinear) equality constraint, and d is the number of (nonlinear) inequality constraints. As a result, the following set of vectors will correspond to the feasible set:

$$A = \{x \in R^n : h(x) = 0, g(x) \leq 0\} \subset R^n$$

The conditions of optimality are set by the *Lagrange* criterion. The Lagrange multipliers for a NLPP with both equality and inequality constraints are defined as:

$$\mathcal{L}(x, \lambda, \mu) = f(x) + \lambda \cdot h(x) + \mu \cdot g(x)$$

In a NLPP, the necessary conditions of optimality are defined by *Karush-Khun-Tucker (KKT)* conditions.[86] If vector x_0 is the optimal solution for the problem, then there exist two multipliers vectors $\lambda \in R^m$ and $\mu \in R^d$ such that:

$$\nabla f(x_0) + \lambda \cdot \nabla h(x_o) + \mu \cdot \nabla g(x_o) = 0,$$

$$h(x_o) = 0$$

$$\mu \cdot g(x_o) = 0$$

$$\mu \geq 0, \ \ g(x_o) \leq 0$$

where $\mu \geq 0$ and $g(x_o) \leq 0$ when the minimum is being found. These conditions are necessary but not sufficient.

There are some important disadvantages about KKT conditions as:
- The system is a nonlinear system.
- A priori, the number of solutions are unknown.
- Every single feasible point is evaluated in the main function $f(x)$.

Sufficient conditions to the problem are:

The feasible set $k = \{x \in R^n : g(x) \leq 0, h(x) = 0\}$ is limited by $\lim_{|x| \to \infty} = +\infty$
- If $f'(\mathbf{x})$ is monotonically increasing, then $f''(\mathbf{x}) > 0$ and $f(\mathbf{x})$ is convex.

The sufficient conditions of optimality require the study of convexity for the function f, g, and the linearity for h constraints.

Every optimal solution of:

$$minimize \ f(\mathbf{x})$$

$$under \ \ h(\mathbf{x}) = 0$$

$$g(\mathbf{x}) \leq 0$$

must be a solution of the system of necessary conditions of optimality (KKT)

$$\nabla f(\mathbf{x}) + \lambda \cdot \nabla h(\mathbf{x}) + \mu \cdot \nabla g(\mathbf{x}) = 0$$

$$\mu \cdot g(\mathbf{x}) = 0$$

$$h(\mathbf{x}) = 0$$

$$\mu \geq 0, \ \ g(\mathbf{x}) \leq 0$$

It is possible to demonstrate that the above conditions are equivalent to[86]:

$$\mu \geq 0, \ \ g(\mathbf{x}) \leq 0$$

$$\mu_i \cdot g(\mathbf{x})_i = 0, \ \ i = 1, 2, \ldots, m$$

It will be required to consider equations and unknown variables to find all the solutions for the KKT conditions:

$$d : inequalities, \ \mu \in R^d$$

$$m : equalities, \ \lambda \in R^m$$

$$n : variables, \ \mathbf{x} \in R^n$$

The solutions of the $d + m + n$ equations with $d + m + n$ unknown variables must be found (there are 2^d cases).

6.4 APPROACH TO THE OPTIMIZATION PROBLEM

The case study presented in Fig. 5.5, has been considered in this section to describe the approach. The occurrence probability associated to each basic event is needed to obtain the Q_{sys}. Therefore, a vector (**q**) collects all the events probabilities together: $\mathbf{q} = [0.02\,0.03\,0.4\,0.08\,0.2\,0.4\,0.09]$. Thus, the Q_{sys} is provided by the BDD is:

$$Q_{sys} = q_1 + q_6 \cdot (1 - q_1) + q_7 \cdot (1 - q_6) \cdot (1 - q_1) + q_5 \cdot q_4 \cdot (1 - q_7) \cdot (1 - q_6)$$
$$\cdot (1 - q_1) + q_3 \cdot q_2 \cdot (1 - q_5) \cdot (1 - q_7) \cdot (1 - q_6) \cdot (1 - q_1) + q_3 \cdot q_2$$
$$\cdot (1 - q_4)(1 - q_7) \cdot (1 - q_6) \cdot (1 - q_1)$$

where, by setting q_n for the corresponding probability, is equal to:

$$Q_{sys} = 47.98\,\%$$

Once the occurrence probability of the top is achieved, the main objective is to reduce it to a certain desired level. The reduction of the Q_{sys} will be done directly by the different events. A new vector **Imp** is defined for that propose as:

$$\mathbf{Imp} = [Imp(e_1)\ Imp(e_2)\ Imp(e_3)\ Imp(e_4)\ Imp(e_5)\ Imp(e_6)\ Imp(e_7)]$$

Therefore, the reduction of Q_{sys} will be done modifying q_i by:

$$
\begin{aligned}
f(Imp(e_n)) = &\ (q_1 - Imp(e_1)) + (q_6 - Imp(e_6)) \cdot (1 - (q_1 - Imp(e_1))) \\
&+ (q_7 - Imp(e_7)) \cdot (1 - (q_6 - Imp(e_6))) \cdot (1 - (q_1 - Imp(e_1))) \\
&+ (q_5 - Imp(e_5)) \cdot (q_4 - Imp(e_4)) \cdot (1 - (q_7 - Imp(e_7))) \\
&\cdot (1 - (q_6 - Imp(e_6))) \cdot (1 - (q_1 - Imp(e_1))) + (q_3 - Imp(e_3)) \\
&\cdot (q_2 - Imp(e_2)) \cdot (1 - (q_5 - Imp(e_5))) \cdot (1 - (q_7 - Imp(e_7))) \\
&\cdot (1 - (q_6 - Imp(e_6))) \cdot (1 - (q_1 - Imp(e_1))) + (q_3 - Imp(e_3)) \\
&\cdot (q_2 - Imp(e_2)) \cdot (1 - (q_4 - Imp(e_4))) \cdot (1 - (q_7 - Imp(e_7))) \\
&\cdot (1 - (q_6 - Imp(e_6))) \cdot (1 - (q_1 - Imp(e_1)))
\end{aligned}
$$

The event e_i has an associated cost related to the improvement $Imp(e_i)$. Therefore, a new vector **Cost** associated with each event improvement is obtained:

$$\mathbf{Cost} = [10000\ 4000\ 8000\ 12000\ 7000\ 5000\ 2000]$$

There is at last an associated budget that is not possible to be exceeded, defined as a scalar. The optimization problem will be:

$$minimize \ f(Imp(e_n))$$

$$under \ \sum_{i=1}^{n} C_i \cdot q_i \leq Budget$$

$$0 \leq Imp(e_i) \leq q_i - a$$

where $f(Imp(e_n))$ is the optimization function; C_i is the cost associated with each event; q_i is the probability assigned to each event; *Budget* is the available budget; a is the parameter for the optimization software that represents the minimum allowable value.

The simulations presented are solved by the *fmincon* function of Matlab.[87] A NLPP *fmincon* in a standard form is:

$$\min_{x} \ f(\boldsymbol{x})$$

$$under \ c(\boldsymbol{x}) \leq 0$$

$$c_{eq}(\boldsymbol{x}) = 0$$

$$\boldsymbol{A} \cdot \boldsymbol{x} \leq b$$

$$\boldsymbol{A}_{eq} \cdot \boldsymbol{x} = \boldsymbol{b}_{eq}$$

$$\boldsymbol{l}_b \leq \boldsymbol{x} \leq \boldsymbol{u}_b$$

where $\mathbf{x}, \mathbf{b}, \mathbf{b_{eq}}, \mathbf{l_b}, \mathbf{u_b}$ are vectors; $\mathbf{A}, \mathbf{A_{eq}}$ are matrices; $f(\mathbf{x})$ is a function that returns a scalar.

fmincon finds a minimum of a constrained nonlinear multivariable function. The syntax used in this simulation is given by:

$$[\boldsymbol{x}, \boldsymbol{fval}, \boldsymbol{exitflag}, \boldsymbol{output}] = fmicom(\boldsymbol{fun}, \boldsymbol{x}_0, \boldsymbol{A}, \boldsymbol{b}, \boldsymbol{lb}, \boldsymbol{up}, options) \qquad (6.1)$$

The function to be optimized need to be set, i.e., to define "fun" function. The CSs and Q_{sys} are defined as in former sections. Fig. 6.3 shows as $f(Imp(e_i))$ is obtained.

Fig. 6.3 Flowchart for $f(Imp(e_i))$.

The parameters for each simulation must be defined when $f(Imp(e_n))$ is set. Initial conditions and boundary conditions must be properly defined. In accordance to the standard definition of a NLPP defined by *fmincon*

- Lower ($\mathbf{l_b}$) and upper ($\mathbf{u_b}$) bounds and **b** must be vectors.
- **A** must be a matrix.

The boundaries vectors $\mathbf{l_b}$ and $\mathbf{u_b}$ are written in the main algorithm. None-theless, two algorithms have been developed to define automatically the constraints to the optimization problem.

Finally, an algorithm creates the matrix related with the inequalities considering the number of variables (n) implicated, i.e., the number of events. Fig. 6.4 shows the flowchart of the algorithm:

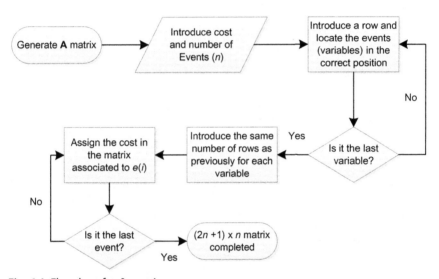

Fig. 6.4 Flowchart for **A** matrix.

The constraints on the left side of the inequality are defined with the information of each variable and its associated cost.

b has the same size as **A**. **b** is defined by Fig. 6.5.

It is achievable regardless of the number of events involved with this information and an explanatory flowchart to simulate a NLPP is provided.

Fig. 6.6 shows the procedure to obtain $\mathbf{x}$, *fval*, *exitflag*, and the output exit variables, where:

- X: new probability associated to each event ($Imp(q_i)$)
- *Fval*: a scalar given by $f(Imp(q_i))$.
- *Exitflag*: will yield the information about the solution accuracy.
- *Output*: solution to the optimization problem.

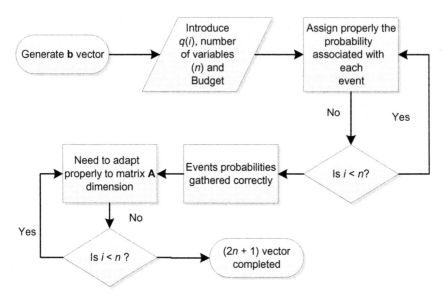

Fig. 6.5 How to generate **b** vector.

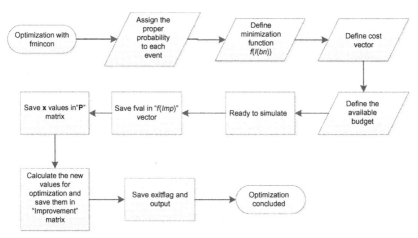

Fig. 6.6 Optimization with *fmincon*.

6.5 EXAMPLE

Let "Tools shortage" be the MP (Top Event) at a certain business, being "Poor work schedule" (e_1), "Limited tools" (e_2), and "Low tools' reliability" (e_3) the events to this problem. Fig. 6.7 shows the LDT.

The CSs from Fig. 6.7 are:

$$CS_1 = e_1$$
$$CS_2 = e_3 \cdot e_2 \cdot \bar{e}_1$$

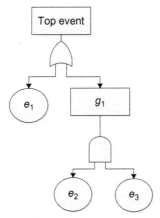

Fig. 6.7 Tools shortage as MP.

Let the probability vector associated be defined as $\mathbf{q} = [0.6\,0.8\,0.9]$. Thus,

$$Q_{sys} = 0.6 + 0.9 \cdot 0.8 \cdot (1 - 0.6) = 0.888$$

The minimization function needed to *fmincon* will be:

$$f(I(b_n)) = [(0.6 - Imp_1) + ((0.9 - Imp_3) \cdot (0.8 - Imp_2) \cdot (1 - (0.6 - Imp_1)))$$

The constraints are given by the budget and the cost vector is as follows:

$$Budget = 200$$

$$\mathbf{Cost} = [1000\,400\,800]$$

The optimization problem is defined as:

$$\text{minimize} \quad (0.6 - I_{b1}) + ((0.9 - I_{b3}) \cdot (0.8 - I_{b2}) \cdot (1 - (0.6 - I_{b1})))$$

$$\text{such that} \quad 1000 \cdot I_{b1} + 400 \cdot I_{b2} + 800 \cdot I_{b3} \le 20000 \quad (4.9)$$

$$0 \le I_{b1} \le 0.6 - 0.001$$

$$0 \le I_{b2} \le 0.8 - 0.001$$

$$0 \le I_{b3} \le 0.9 - 0.001$$

The Lagrangian to this problem is given by:

$$L(Imp_1, Imp_2, Imp_3, \mu_1, \mu_2, \mu_3, \mu_4, \mu_5, \mu_6, \mu_7)$$
$$= (0.6 - Imp_1) + ((0.9 - Imp_3) \cdot (0.8 - Imp_2) \cdot (1 - (0.6 - Imp_1))) + \mu_1$$
$$\cdot (-Imp_1) + \mu_2 \cdot (-Imp_2) + \mu_3 \cdot (-Imp_3) + \mu_4 \cdot (Imp_1 - 0.6) + \mu_5$$
$$\cdot (Imp_2 - 0.8) + \mu_6 \cdot (Imp_3 - 0.9) + \mu_7$$
$$\cdot (1000 \cdot Imp_1 + 400 \cdot Imp_2 + 800 \cdot Imp_3 - 200)$$

Considering the KKT optimal conditions:

$$\nabla f(x) + \sum_{i=0}^{d} \mu_i \cdot \nabla g(x)_i = 0$$

$$\sum_{i=0}^{d} \mu_i \cdot \nabla g(x)_i = 0$$

$$\mu \geq 0, g(x) \leq 0$$

writing down the KKT conditions:

$$(0.9 - Imp_3) \cdot (0.8 - Imp_2) \cdot 2 - 1 - m_1 = 0$$
$$(0.6 - Imp_3) \cdot (1 - (0.6 - Imp_1)) \cdot (-1) - m_2 = 0$$
$$(0.8 - Imp_2) \cdot (1 - (0.6 - Imp_1)) \cdot (-1) - m_3 = 0$$
$$m_1 \cdot Imp_1 = 0$$
$$m_2 \cdot Imp_2 = 0$$
$$m_3 \cdot Imp_3 = 0$$
$$m_4 \cdot (Imp_1 - 0.6) = 0$$
$$m_5 \cdot (Imp_2 - 0.8) = 0$$
$$m_6 \cdot (Imp_3 - 0.9) = 0$$
$$m_7 \cdot (1000 \cdot Imp_1 + 400 \cdot Imp_2 + 800 \cdot Imp_3 - 200) = 0$$

where there are ten equations and ten unknown variables, considering that the constraints of the multipliers must be $\mu_i \geq 0$.

Therefore, 2^d cases, being d the number of inequalities, must be studied and analyzed to find the optimal solution. Every feasible value should be evaluated in the main function to obtain the minimum.

There are different methods to solve this NLPP. This case has no difficulty, being possible to solve it by hand-calculations. Nonetheless, larger LDTs with a great number of events could be found in a real case scenario where the computational cost is high. The feasible solutions found by *fmincon* are:

$$Imp_1 = 0$$

$$Imp_2 = 0.5$$

$$Imp_3 = 0$$

i.e., the business should invest $0.5 \cdot 400 = 200$ € for reducing the probability of the second event from 0.8 to 0.3.

Table 6.1 presents the improvement in the occurrence probabilities of each event according to the investment and the associated cost.

Table 6.1 Data obtained after optimization

	Initial q_n	q_n after optimization	Cost associated	Investment
e_1	60%	60%	1000 €	0 €
e_2	80%	30%	400 €	200 €
e_3	90%	90%	800 €	0 €

If an investment of 200 € is done for reducing the occurrence probability of the second event (e_2), the MP probability of occurrence will be reduced from 88% to 70%. According to the solution found, the business might improve its "Tools Shortage" problem and to reduce its occurrence probability when they invest 200 € in the basic cause "Limited tools." A higher budget should be assigned to each event if the business requires a major improvement in the reduction of the occurrence probability of the top event.

6.6 DYNAMIC ANALYSIS AND OPTIMIZATION

Fig. 6.8 presents the flowchart of the optimization algorithm. The algorithm evaluates the main function regarding the initial conditions. When the feasible solutions are obtained, then they are recorded as:

- **P** is the feasible solutions of the NLPP, i.e., **x** values given after the optimization.
- *Improvement matrix* contains the updated probabilities of each BC.
- **f(Imp)** vector is the main function evaluated in the feasible points given by the NLPP.

fmincon is employed to find the optimal solution, or at least, a good solution. The algorithm set the simulations when the feasible points are obtained and recorded in the aforementioned variables.

The main purpose of the dynamic analysis is to study the gradual reduction of the occurrence probability of the top event with a certain degree of confidence. The algorithm is capable to stop the simulation when a certain threshold is reached. It provides the resources that should be invested to obtain a certain occurrence probability of the top event in a period.

Fig. 6.9 shows the flowchart including the threshold limit.

6.7 EXAMPLE

The case study presented in Fig. 6.7 is solved considering a period of four months. The first month approach is the same. The solutions of the iteration "t" are used as initial conditions for the iteration "$t+1$."

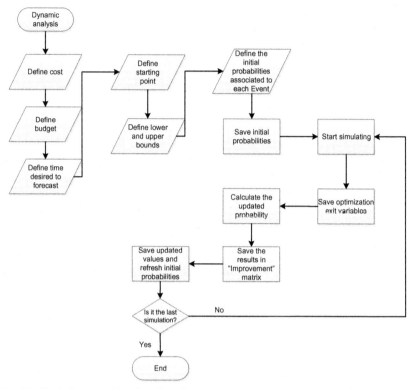

Fig. 6.8 Optimization algorithm flowchart.

The initial values/conditions are:

$$f(I(b_n)) = [(0.6 - Imp_{e1})$$
$$+((0.9 - Imp_{e3}) \cdot (0.8 - Imp_{e2}) \cdot (1 - (0.6 - Imp_{e1})))$$

$$W = [0.6\,0.8\,0.9]$$

$$Cost = [1000\,400\,800]$$

$$Budget = 200$$

The initial occurrence probability of the Top Event is $Q_{sys} = 88.8\%$. A simulation over the first month is achieved. Then the variables defined in this algorithm are given by:

$$Improvement = [0.6\,0.3\,0.9]$$

$$P = [0\,0.5\,0]$$

$$f(Imp) = 70.8\%$$

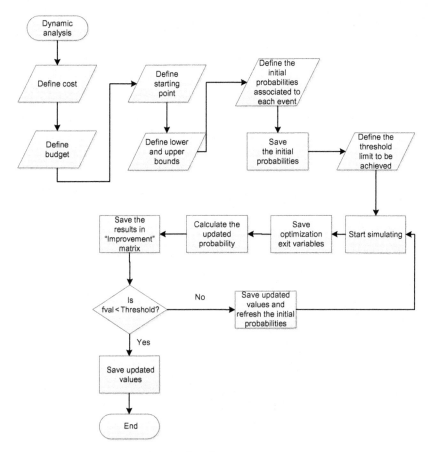

Fig. 6.9 Threshold limit simulations flowchart.

The variables will be updated in each iteration over the time. The feasible points will form the new vector of probabilities to be optimized. The approach that will provide a reduction of the occurrence probability of the Top Event requires:

- The cost required.
- The months to reduce the probability to a certain level.
- The resources allocation of the business.

There will be some cases where the MP cannot be completely removed, i.e., only a reasonable level of reduction can be achieved.

Table 6.2 shows the optimized values of each event, i.e., **P** matrix (the probability reduction values).

Table 6.2 Probability reduction

	1st month	2nd month	3rd month	4th month
Imp1	0	0.08	0.20	0.20
Imp2	0.50	0.30	0	0
Imp3	0	0	0	0

Fig. 6.10 shows the probability reduction of the events over the time. The second event (e_2) has the most important reduction in the first and the second months. It is for the first event (e_1) in the third month. It can be also observed that the approach raises the value of the first event, being close to 20% during the third and fourth months.

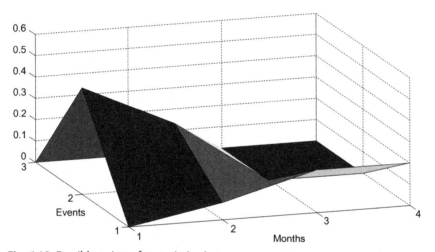

Fig. 6.10 Feasible points after optimization.

The new probability values are presented in Table 6.3.

Table 6.3 Probabilities for the optimization of each event

	Initial	1st month	2nd month	3rd month	4th month
Probability e_1	0.60	0.60	0.52	0.32	0.12
Probability e_2	0.80	0.30	0	0	0
Probability e_3	0.90	0.90	0.90	0.90	0.90

Fig. 6.11 shows the updated probability of the events over the time. In the first month, the probability of e_2 is drastically reduced. Then, the probability of e_1 is reduced and the probability of e_3 does not change over the period in the following months.

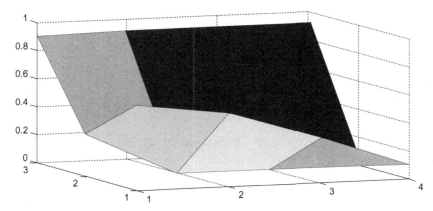

Fig. 6.11 Events improvement.

Table 6.4 shows the values obtained by $f(Imp)$, i.e., the probability of the MP over the period considered.

Table 6.4 MP probability of occurrence

Q_{sys}	Initial	1st month	2nd month	3rd month	4th month
$f(Imp)$	88.8%	70.92%	52.14%	32.16%	12.17%

The initial probability of occurrence for "Tools Shortage" was around 88%. After a few iterations, the algorithm states that a reduction of the occurrence probability from 88% to 12% can be achieved if the resources of the business are allocated as Tables 6.3 and 6.5. The distribution of the budget would be:

Table 6.5 Costs considering the optimization solution

	1st month	2nd month	3rd month	4th month
Investment e_1	0 €	80 €	200 €	200 €
Investment e_2	200 €	120 €	0 €	0 €
Investment e_3	0 €	0 €	0 €	0 €

The outcomes of *fmincon* are:
- Optimization terminated: "first-order optimality measure less than *options. TolFun* and maximum constraint violation is less than *options. TolCon*"
- *Exitflag* = 1
- *Iterations* = 2
- *FuncCount* = 12
- *Firstorderoptimality* = 2.2204×10^{-16}

The algorithm developed can minimize the probability of occurrence of a particular LDT by allocating the business resources optimally. With this approach, the business will be able to:

- Set the best allocation of resources each month to reduce the occurrence probability of the Top Event.
- Have under control the events which lead to a certain problem (Top Event) in the business.
- Have a certain degree of confidence in the investment done in each event.

6.8 Real Case Study

Fig. 5.1 shows a LDT related to a real case study of a confidential firm. Table 6.6 details the initial conditions. Fig. 5.2 BDD obtained from Fig. 5.1 presents the BDD obtained from this LDT.

The probability of occurrence of the MP is 0.4825, calculated by using the analytical expression from Fig. 5.2 and the probabilities of Table 6.6. The maximum investment (MI) is:

$$MI = 0.4 \times 0.9 \times 500 + 0.4 \times 0.5 \times 150 + 0.2 \times 0.4 \times 400 + 0.3 \times 0.9$$
$$\times 400 + 0.1 \times 0.8 \times 150 + 0.2 \times 0.5 \times 200 + 0.25 \times 0.6 \times 500 + 0.2$$
$$\times 0.3 \times 300 + 0.1 \times 0.95 \times 900$$
$$= 560.5$$

Fig. 6.12 shows the maximum investment for each BC.

If this maximum budget were available, then the minimum probabilities of occurrence (P_{min}) of the BCs will be:

$$P_{min} = [0.04 \quad 0.20 \quad 0.12 \quad 0.03 \quad 0.020 \quad 0.10 \quad 0.10 \quad 0.14 \quad 0.005]$$

and, consequently, the minimum Q_{MP} is:

$$Q_{MP} = 0.1329$$

Therefore, when the available budget is less than 560.5 monetary units (mu), it will be necessary to choose the BCs that are the best to be improved in order to minimize the Q_{MP}.

The budget considered in the following example is 350 mu. For this purpose, the problem to optimize will be:

$$minimize \quad Q_{MP}(Imp(BC))$$

Table 6.6 Case study: initial conditions

Description	Notation	Probability of occurrence	IC (Monetary units)	Improvement limit (a)
BUDGET 350				
Customer complaints	MP	–	–	–
Errors from the quality control department	Cause 1	–	–	–
Lack of training	Cause 2	–	–	–
No internal training is provided	BC1	40%	500	90%
Lack of necessary equipment	BC2	40%	150	50%
Failures in protocols	Cause 3	–	–	–
Review protocols are not well defined	BC3	20%	400	40%
Absenteeism training courses	BC4	30%	400	90%
Errors from the logistics department	Cause 4	–	–	–
Problems in the distribution	Cause 5	–	–	–
Poorly optimized distribution	Cause 6	–	–	–
Poorly established routes	BC5	10%	150	80%
Forecast problems	BC6	20%	200	50%
Driving inappropriate for fragile products	BC7	25%	500	60%
Problems in stores	Cause 7	–	–	–
Improperly stored products	BC8	20%	300	30%
Obsolete warehouse	BC9	10%	900	95%

subject to

$$(500 \cdot Imp(BC_1) + 150 \cdot Imp(BC_2) + 400 \cdot Imp(BC_3) + 400 \cdot Imp(BC_4)$$
$$+ 150 \cdot Imp(BC_5) + 200 \cdot Imp(BC_6) + 500 \cdot Imp(BC_7) + 300$$
$$\cdot Imp(BC_8) + 900 \cdot Imp(BC_9)) \cdot 10$$
$$\leq 350$$

$$Imp(BC_1) - 0.36 \leq 0; \quad -Imp(BC_1) \leq 0$$

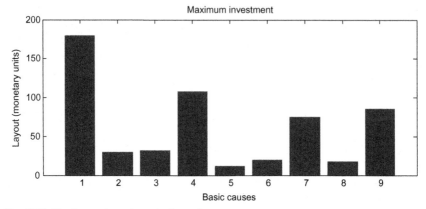

Fig. 6.12 Maximum investment allowed.

$$Imp(BC_2) - 0.2 \leq 0; \quad -Imp(BC_2) \leq 0$$
$$Imp(BC_3) - 0.12 \leq 0; \quad -Imp(BC_3) \leq 0$$
$$Imp(BC_4) - 0.27 \leq 0; \quad -Imp(BC_4) \leq 0$$
$$Imp(BC_5) - 0.08 \leq 0; \quad -Imp(BC_5) \leq 0$$
$$Imp(BC_6) - 0.1 \leq 0; \quad -Imp(BC_6) \leq 0$$
$$Imp(BC_7) - 0.2 \leq 0; \quad -Imp(BC_4) \leq 0$$
$$Imp(BC_8) - 0.06 \leq 0; \quad -Imp(BC_5) \leq 0$$
$$Imp(BC_9) - 0.095 \leq 0; \quad -Imp(BC_6) \leq 0$$

Fig. 6.13 shows the optimal investment allocation subject to a budget of 350 mu to minimize Q_{MP}.

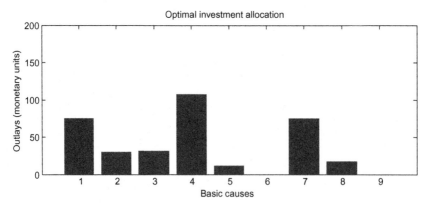

Fig. 6.13 Optimal investment.

There are 2 BCs that cannot be improved due to the fact that budget is limited, and there are 3 BCs whose maximum investments are not completed. The missing amounts to invest are:

$$BC_1 = 105\,\text{mu}, BC_6 = 20\,\text{mu}, BC_9 = 85\,\text{mu}$$

Fig. 6.14 shows the behavior of the Q_{MP} reduction according to the available budget. The Q_{MP} presents a nonlinear behavior.

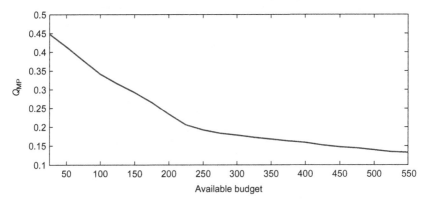

Fig. 6.14 Optimal investment allocation.

Fig. 6.15 shows the improvement of each investment compared to the previous one. The investment considered rises with a step of 50 mu.

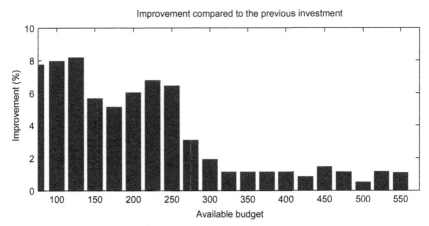

Fig. 6.15 Percentage improvement.

The slope is more pronounced at the beginning (Fig. 6.14). The first 250 mu are more useful than the rest of the investment (Fig. 6.15). This is useful information when the availability of budget is limited.

Annex A: Boolean Algebra

Idempotent:

$$A + A = A \qquad (A.1)$$

$$A \cdot A = A \qquad (A.2)$$

Involution:

$$\bar{\bar{A}} = A \qquad (A.3)$$

Commutative addition:

$$A + B = B + A \qquad (A.4)$$

Commutative product:

$$A \cdot B = B \cdot A \qquad (A.5)$$

Associative addition:

$$A + (B + C) = A + (B + C) \qquad (A.6)$$

Associative product:

$$A \cdot (B \cdot C) = A \cdot (B \cdot C) \qquad (A.7)$$

Distributive addition:

$$A + (B \cdot C) = (A + B) \cdot (A + C) \qquad (A.8)$$

Distributive product

$$A \cdot (B + C) = (A \cdot B) + (A \cdot C) \qquad (A.9)$$

Absorption rules:

$$A + (A \cdot B) = A \qquad (A.10)$$

$$A \cdot (A + B) = A \qquad (A.11)$$

De Morgan's rules:

$$\overline{A + B} = \bar{A} + \bar{B} \qquad (A.12)$$

$$\overline{A \cdot B} = \bar{A} \cdot \bar{B} \qquad (A.13)$$

Axioms:

$$0 + A = A \tag{A.14}$$

$$1 + A = 1 \tag{A.15}$$

$$0 \cdot A = 0 \tag{A.16}$$

$$1 \cdot A = 0 \tag{A.17}$$

Principle of duality:

All logical relations will have a dual one. The dual expression is to change unions for intersections and 1 for 0.

Theorem of functions

Any function can be decomposed depending on its variables and according to the following relation:

$$f(A, B, C, \ldots) = A \cdot f(1, B, C, \ldots) + \bar{A} \cdot f(0, B, C, \ldots),$$

where $f(1, B, C, \ldots)$ is the resulting function when A is valued as 1 and $\bar{A}$ is valued as 0. The second term $f(0, B, C, \ldots)$ is the resulting function when A is valued as 0 and $\bar{A}$ is valued as 1.

De Morgan's generalized laws:

The complementary function is obtained using the complementary variables and exchanging sums and products. This can be expressed as:

$$\overline{f(A, B, C, \ldots, +, i)} = f(\bar{A}, \bar{B}, \bar{C}, \ldots \bar{i})$$

Annex B: Symbology of the Logical Decision Tree

Symbol	Name	Description
○	BASIC EVENT	Event that cannot be broken down into more elementary events
▭	INTERMEDIATE EVENT	Event that occurs due to previous occurrence of other causes. It can be broken down into more elementary events
⬭	CONDITIONAL EVENT	Conditions or constraints that are applied to an Inhibition gate or a Priority AND
◇	NON-DEVELOPED EVENT	Event that is not developed into more complex events because its consequences are despicable or there is not enough information
⌂	EXTERNAL EVENT	Event that usually occurs. It is usually constant and can adopt only one logical value (1 or 0)
AND gate	AND	Logical product operator: The output event only occurs when all the input events occur
OR gate	OR	Logical sum operator: The output event occurs if, at least, one of the input events occur
VOTE gate k/n	VOTE (k out of n)	The output event occurs if, at least, k out of n input events occur

Continued

—cont'd

Symbol	Name	Description
	INHIBITION GATE	The output event occurs if a specific condition occurs
	NOT	The output event is the negation of the input event
	INPUT TRANSFER	The LDT is continues where this symbol appears again
	OUTPUT TRANSFER	This connection indicates that an event goes out of the LDT. This position must be related to the input transfer
	EXCLUSIVE OR	The output event occurs if the input occurs in a specific order activated by a certain condition
	PRIORITY AND	The output event occurs if only one of the input events occur
SEQ	SEQ GATE	The output event occurs if the inputs occur in a specific sequence
CSP	SPARE GATE	If the event C occurs, it will be replaced by reserve events
FDEP	FUNCTIONAL DEPENDENCE	When the shot event occurs, the basic dependent events are forced to happen

Annex C: Probability Theory

C.1 NOMENCLATURE

Random experiment: The result is not known in advance but there is a set of possible results.

Sample space: It is the set of possible results of a random experiment.

An *event* is the result or set of results of an experiment, therefore, it can be defined as a specific subset of a sample space. The main types of events are:

- *True event*: It is an event that always happens. The associated subset is the entire sample space.
- *Impossible event*: It never occurs as a result of an experiment. The associated subset is the empty set.
- *Identical events*: They are events that can occur simultaneously for each observation or experiment.
- *Complementary event*: It is an event that occurs if its complementary event does not occur and *vice versa*.
- *Incompatible events*: They are events that cannot occur simultaneously.
- *Dependent events*: The occurrence of an event A is conditioned by the occurrence of another event B.
- *Complementary event*: The complementary event of an event A occurs when A does not occur.

$$\bar{A} : \{x : x \notin A\}$$
$$P(\bar{A}) = 1 - P(A)$$

- *Intersection*: The intersection of two events A, B is other event, or events, belonging to A and B simultaneously.
$$A \cap B : \{(x \in A) y (x \in B)\}$$
- *Union*: The union of A and B is other event (or events) belonging to A, B, or both of them:
$$A \cup B : \{(x \in A) or (x \in B)\}$$

C.2 USEFUL RELATIONS

The probability of occurrence of the top event can be achieved in the evaluation of LDTs as the probability of the union of all the CSs.

C.2.1 Inclusion-Exclusion Principle

The probability of the union of a set "N" with n elements can be calculated as follows:

$$P\left(\cup_{i=1}^n A_i\right) = \sum_{1 \leq i \leq n} P(A_i) - \sum_{1 \leq i < j \leq n} P(A_i \cap A_j)$$
$$+ \sum_{1 \leq i < j < k \leq n} P(A_i \cap A_j \cap A_K) + \cdots + (-1)^{n+1} P(A_i \cap A_j \ldots \cap A_n)$$

(C.1)

Eq. (C.1) can be expressed as:

$$P\left(\cup_{i=1}^n A_i\right) = \sum_{k=1}^n (-1)^{n+1} \cdot S_k \tag{C.2}$$

where each factor S_k is a sum of probabilities of intersections of k-tuples, subsets of N forming all the possible combinations of k elements:

$$S_K = \sum_{\{J:J \subseteq N, |J|=k\}} P\left(\cap_{j \in J} A_j\right)$$

Each S_k contains:

$$\binom{n}{k} = \frac{n!}{(n-k)!k!} \text{ terms.}$$

This formula can be truncated in a summation of terms of even-order or odd-order terms. Thus, *Bonferroni's inequalities* are obtained as:

$$P\left(\cup_{i=1}^n A_i\right) \geq S_1 - S_2 + \cdots + (-1)^{n+1} S_K, \quad \text{for } k \text{ even} \tag{C.2a}$$
$$P\left(\cup_{i=1}^n A_i\right) \leq S_1 - S_2 + \cdots + (-1)^{n+1} S_K, \quad \text{for } k \text{ odd} \tag{C.2b}$$

C.2.2 Rare Event Approximation

If the probabilities of the events are very low, then the inclusion–exclusion formula can be truncated avoiding the high order terms. This is the *rare-event approximation* that is reduced to the sum of the probabilities.

$$P\left(\cup_{i=1}^n C_i\right) \cong P_{\text{RareEvent}} = \sum_{1 \leq i \leq n} P(C_i) \tag{C.3}$$

C.2.3 Upper Bond Approximation

The De Morgan's theorem is used to obtain the probability of the union of events. The probability of occurrence of the top event can be expressed as:

$$f = \cup_{i=1}^n C_i = C_1 + C_2 + \cdots + C_n \tag{C.4}$$

The probability that the top event does not occur can be calculated by the product of the complementary probabilities of occurrence of the events.

$$Q_{\text{Nonocurrence}} = \prod_{i=1}^{n}(1 - q_i)$$

Then, the probability of occurrence is obtained as (Fig. C.1):

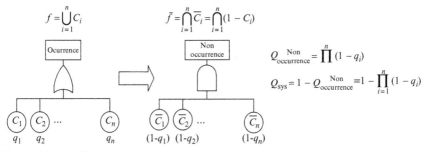

Fig. C.1 Probability of the union of events using the Upper Bond approximation.

$$Q_{\text{Sys}} = 1 - Q_{\text{Nonocurrence}} = 1 - \prod_{i=1}^{n}(1 - q_i) \qquad (C.5)$$

The expression for the Upper–Bond approximation is:

$$P\left(\cup_{i=1}^{n} A_i\right) \stackrel{\approx}{=} P_{\text{UpperBond}} = 1 - \prod_{i=1}^{n}(1 - P(A_i)) \qquad (C.6)$$

being:

$$P\left(\cup_{i=1}^{n} A_i\right) = P_{\text{Incl-Excl}} \leq P_{\text{UpperBond}} \leq P_{\text{RareEven}} \qquad (C.7)$$

C.2.4 Probability for a *k*-out of-*n*

A useful value is the probability in the output of a VOTE gate (*k* out of *n*). This probability is:

$$P_{koutofn} = \sum_{j=k}^{n}(-1)^{j-n} \cdot \binom{j-1}{k-1} \cdot S_j \qquad (C.8)$$

C.2.5 Independent Events

If the information provided by an event A does not modify the occurrence of the event B, then these events are independent. Thus, A and B are independent if:

$$P(A \cap B) = P(A) \cdot P(B) \qquad (C.9)$$

C.2.6 Conditioned Probability

It is important to know if the occurrence of an event A provides information about the occurrence of B when a random experiment is carried out. The conditional probability aims to solve this problem.

Given a sample space and an event A with $P(A) > 0$, the probability of B conditioned by A, $P(B/A)$, is defined as:

$$P(B/A) = \frac{P(A \cap B)}{P(A)} \tag{C.10}$$

C.2.7 Composed Probabilities Theorem

Given a simple space and the events A and B, with $P(A) > 0$ and $P(B) > 0$, then:

$$P(A \cap B) = P(A) \cdot P(B/A) = P(B) \cdot P(A/B) \tag{C.11}$$

This theorem allows calculating the probability of conditioned events.

C.2.8 Total Probability Theorem

If $\{A\}_{i \in N}$ is a complete system and $P(A_i) > 0$ for each $i \in N$, then if an event B is given as:

$$P(B) = \sum_{i=1}^{\infty} P(A) \cdot P(B/A_i) \tag{C.12}$$

C.2.9 Bayes's Theorem

If $\{A\}_{i \in N}$ is a complete system and $P(A_i) > 0$ for each $i \in N$ and B is $P(B) > 0$, therefore:

$$P(A_i/B) = \frac{P(A_i).P(B/A_i)}{\sum_{i=1}^{\infty} P(A_i) \cdot P(B/A_i)} \tag{C.13}$$

The last two theorems are valid if the family of events (A_i) is finite. The probabilities of A are called "a priori" probabilities, the A_i/B probabilities are called "a posteriori", and B/A_i are called "*verisimilitude*".

Annex D: Importance Analysis: Practical Cases

CASE 1

The Top Event of this LDT is given by the following logical function (Fig. D.1):

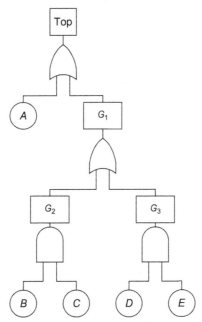

Fig. D.1 LDT without MOEs.

$$f = A + BC + DE$$

The MCSs are:

$$CMS_1 = A$$
$$CMS_2 = BC$$
$$CMS_3 = DE$$

The probability of occurrence of the Top Event of the union of the cut sets. This probability is calculated using the Inclusion-Exclusion Principle:

$$Q_{sys} = P(A \cup BC \cup DE)$$
$$= P(A) + P(BC) + P(DE) - P(A \cap BC) - P(A \cap DE)$$
$$- P(BC \cap DE) + P(A \cap BC \cap DE)$$

$$Q_{sys} = q_A + q_B q_C + q_D q_E - q_A q_B q_C - q_A q_D q_E - q_B q_C q_D q_E + q_A q_B q_C q_D q_E$$

Assuming a constant probability of occurrence for all the events $q_A = q_B = q_C = q_D = q_E = 0.01$, the probability of occurrence of the Top Event is:

$$Q_{sys} = 0.01 + 2(0.01)^2 - 2(0.01)^3 - (0.01)^4 + 0.01^5 = 0.010198$$

Fussell-Vesely

$$I_A^{FV} = \frac{P(A)}{Q_{sys}} = \frac{q_A}{Q_{sys}} = \frac{0.01}{0.010198} = 0.980584$$

$$I_B^{FV} = I_C^{FV} = \frac{P(BC)}{Q_{sys}} = \frac{q_B q_C}{Q_{sys}} = \frac{0.01^2}{0.010198} = 0.009806$$

$$I_D^{FV} = I_E^{FV} = \frac{P(DE)}{Q_{sys}} = \frac{q_D q_E}{Q_{sys}} = \frac{0.01^2}{0.010198} = 0.009806$$

Birnbaum

The derivative is:

$$Q_{sys} = q_A + q_B q_C + q_D q_E - q_A q_B q_C - q_A q_D q_E - q_B q_C q_D q_E$$

then:

$$I_A^{Birm} = \frac{\partial Q_{sys}}{\partial q_A} = 1 - q_B q_C - q_D q_E + q_B q_C q_D q_E = 1 - 2(0.01)^2 + 0.01^4$$

$$= 0.9998$$

$$I_B^{Birm} = \frac{\partial Q_{sys}}{\partial q_B} = q_C - q_A q_C - q_C q_D q_E + q_A q_C q_D q_E$$

$$= 0.01 - (0.010)^2 - (0.01)^3 + 0.01^4 = 0.0099$$

$$I_C^{Birm} = I_D^{Birm} = I_E^{Birm} = 0.0099$$

AND Criterion

The following ranking is obtained considering the number of the AND gates until reaching the top for each event.

Rank	Events	AND gates
1.	A	0
2.	B	1
2.	C	1
2.	D	1
2.	E	1

Heuristic Structural Criterion

The list of variables from the TDLR method is: A, B, C, D, and E. With regard to the LDT of Fig. D.2, then:

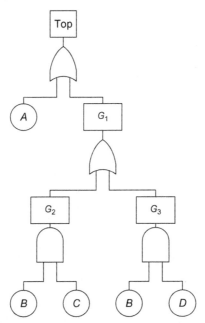

Fig. D.2 LDT with one MOE.

Event A:

(1) Being $q_A = 1$, $q_i = \dfrac{1}{2}\ \forall i \neq A$

Level 3 (AND gates): $G_2 = \dfrac{1}{2}\cdot\dfrac{1}{2} = \dfrac{1}{4}$; $G_3 = \dfrac{1}{2}\cdot\dfrac{1}{2} = \dfrac{1}{4}$

Level 2 (OR gate): $G_1 = 1 - \left[\left(1 - \dfrac{1}{4}\right)\left(1 - \dfrac{1}{4}\right)\right] = 7/16$

Level 1 (OR gate): $Top = 1 - \left[(1 - 1)\left(1 - \dfrac{7}{16}\right)\right] = 1$

(2) Considering $q_A = 0$, $q_i = \dfrac{1}{2} \forall i \neq A$

Level 3 (AND gates): $G_2 = \dfrac{1}{2} \cdot \dfrac{1}{2} = \dfrac{1}{4}$; $G_3 = \dfrac{1}{2} \cdot \dfrac{1}{2} = \dfrac{1}{4}$

Level 2 (OR gate): $G_1 = 1 - \left[\left(1 - \dfrac{1}{4}\right)\left(1 - \dfrac{1}{4}\right) \right] = 7/16$

Level 1 (OR gate): $Top = 1 - \left[(1 - 0)\left(1 - \dfrac{7}{16}\right) \right] = 7/16$

being: $I_A^{Struc} = 1 - \dfrac{7}{16} = 9/16$

Event B:

(1) Taking into account: $q_B = 1$, $q_i = \dfrac{1}{2} \forall i \neq B$

Level 3 (AND gates): $G_2 = 1 \cdot \dfrac{1}{2} = \dfrac{1}{2}$; $G_3 = \dfrac{1}{2} \cdot \dfrac{1}{2} = \dfrac{1}{4}$

Level 2 (OR gate): $G_1 = 1 - \left[\left(1 - \dfrac{1}{2}\right)\left(1 - \dfrac{1}{2}\right) \right] = 5/8$

Level 1 (OR gate): $Top = 1 - \left[\left(1 - \dfrac{1}{2}\right)\left(1 - \dfrac{5}{8}\right) \right] = 13/16$

(2) Being $q_B = 1$, $q_i = \dfrac{1}{2} \forall i \neq B$

Level 3 (AND gates): $G_2 = 0 \cdot \dfrac{1}{2} = 0$; $G_3 = \dfrac{1}{2} \cdot \dfrac{1}{2} = \dfrac{1}{4}$

Level 2 (OR gate): $G_1 = 1 - \left[(1 - 0)\left(1 - \dfrac{1}{4}\right) \right] = 1/4$

Level 1 (OR gate): $Top = 1 - \left[\left(1 - \dfrac{1}{2}\right)\left(1 - \dfrac{1}{4}\right) \right] = 5/8$

where $I_B^{Struc} = \dfrac{13}{16} - \dfrac{5}{8} = 3/16$

For the events C, D, and E, then $I_C^{Struc} = I_D^{Struc} = I_E^{Struc} = 3/16$

CASE 2

The Top Event of this LDT is given by the following logical function:

$$f = A + BC + BD$$

The MCSs are:

$$CMS_1 = A$$

$$CMS_2 = BC$$

$$CMS_3 = BD$$

The probability of occurrence of the Top Event is:

$$
\begin{aligned}
Q_{sys} &= P(A \cup BC \cup BD) \\
&= P(A) + P(BC) + P(BD) - P(A \cap BC) - P(A \cap BD) \\
&\quad - P(BC \cap BD) + P(A \cap BC \cap BD)
\end{aligned}
$$

Assuming that all the events are independent, then:

$$Q_{sys} = q_A + q_B q_C + q_B q_D - q_A q_B q_C - q_A q_B q_D - q_B q_C q_D + q_A q_B q_C q_D$$

the probability of occurrence of the Top Event for $q_A = q_B = q_C = q_D = 0.01$ is:

$$Q_{sys} = 0.01 + 2(0.01)^2 - 3(0.01)^3 + 0.01^4 = 0.010197$$

Fussell-Vesely

$$I_A^{FV} = \frac{P(A)}{Q_{sys}} = \frac{q_A}{Q_{sys}} = \frac{0.01}{0.010198} = 0.98068$$

$$
\begin{aligned}
I_B^{FV} &= \frac{P(BC \cup BD)}{Q_{sys}} = \frac{P(BC) + P(BD) - P(BC \cap BD)}{Q_{sys}} \\
&= \frac{q_B q_C + q_B q_D - q_B q_C q_D}{Q_{sys}} = 2(0.01)^2 - 0.01^3 = 0.019516
\end{aligned}
$$

$$I_C^{FV} = \frac{P(BC)}{Q_{sys}} = \frac{q_B q_C}{Q_{sys}} = \frac{0.01^2}{0.010197} = 0.009807$$

$$I_D^{FV} = \frac{P(BD)}{Q_{sys}} = \frac{q_B q_D}{Q_{sys}} = \frac{0.01^2}{0.010197} = 0.009807$$

Birnbaum

The derivative is given by:

$$Q_{sys} = q_A + q_B q_C + q_B q_D - q_A q_B q_C - q_A q_B q_D - q_B q_C q_D + q_A q_B q_C q_D$$

being:

$$I_A^{Birm} = \frac{\partial Q_{sys}}{\partial q_A} = 1 - q_B q_C - q_B q_D + q_B q_C q_D = 1 - 2(0.01)^2 + 0.1^3 = 0.9998$$

$$
\begin{aligned}
I_B^{Birm} &= \frac{\partial Q_{sys}}{\partial q_B} = q_C + q_D - q_A q_C - q_A q_D - q_C q_D + q_A q_C q_D \\
&= 2(0.01) - 3(0.01)^2 + 0.1^3 = 0.0197
\end{aligned}
$$

$$I_C^{\text{Birm}} = \frac{\partial Q_{\text{sys}}}{\partial q_C} = q_B + q_A q_B - q_A q_D + q_A q_B q_D = 0.01 - 2(0.01)^2 + 0.1^3$$
$$= 0.0098$$

$$I_D^{\text{Birm}} = \frac{\partial Q_{\text{sys}}}{\partial q_D} = q_B + q_A q_B - q_B q_C + q_A q_B q_C = 0.01 - 2(0.01)^2 + 0.1^3$$
$$= 0.0098$$

AND Criterion

This LDT has a MOE (event B) placed in two different nodes of the tree. The number of AND gates must be counted for these two locations and the node with less AND gates must be considered. Therefore, the ranking of events will be:

Rank	Sucesos	Puertas AND
1.	A	0
2.	B	1
2.	C	1
2.	D	1

Heuristic Structural Criterion

The variable ranking according to the TDLR method is: A, B, C, D, and E. The LDT of Fig. D.3 has been considered in the following calculus.

Event A:

(1) Considering $q_A = 1$, $\quad q_i = \frac{1}{2} \forall i \neq A$

Level 3 (AND gates): $G_2 = \frac{1}{2} \cdot \frac{1}{2} = \frac{1}{4}; \quad G_3 = \frac{1}{2} \cdot \frac{1}{2} = \frac{1}{4}$

Level 2 (OR gate): $G_1 = 1 - \left[\left(1 - \frac{1}{4}\right)\left(1 - \frac{1}{4}\right) \right] = \frac{7}{16}$

Level 1 (OR gate): $Top = 1 - \left[(1-1)\left(1 - \frac{7}{16}\right) \right] = 1$

(2) Taking into account $q_A = 0$, $\quad q_i = \frac{1}{2} \forall i \neq A$

Level 3 (AND gates): $G_2 = \frac{1}{2} \cdot \frac{1}{2} = \frac{1}{4}; \quad G_3 = \frac{1}{2} \cdot \frac{1}{2} = \frac{1}{4}$

Level 2 (OR gate): $G_1 = 1 - \left[\left(1 - \frac{1}{4}\right)\left(1 - \frac{1}{4}\right) \right] = 7/16$

Level 1 (OR gate): $Top = 1 - \left[(1-1)\left(1 - \frac{7}{16}\right) \right] = 1$

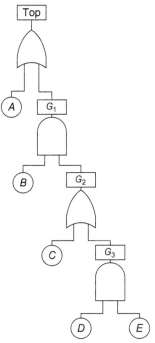

Fig. D.3 LDT with two AND gates at different levels.

being: $I_A^{Struc} = 1 - \dfrac{7}{16} = 9/16$

Event B:

(1) Being $q_B = 1$, $q_i = \dfrac{1}{2} \, \forall i \neq B$

Level 3 (AND gates): $G_2 = 1 \cdot \dfrac{1}{2} = \dfrac{1}{2}$; $G_3 = 1 \cdot \dfrac{1}{2} = \dfrac{1}{2}$

Level 2 (OR gate): $G_1 = 1 - \left[\left(1 - \dfrac{1}{4}\right) \left(1 - \dfrac{1}{4}\right) \right] = 7/16$

Level 1 (OR gate): $Top = 1 - \left[(1 - 1)\left(1 - \dfrac{7}{16}\right) \right] = 1$

(2) Taking into account $q_B = 0$, $q_i = \dfrac{1}{2} \, \forall i \neq B$

Level 3 (AND gates): $G_2 = 0 \cdot \dfrac{1}{2} = 0$; $G_3 = 0 \cdot \dfrac{1}{2} = 0$

Level 2 (OR gate): $G_1 = 1 - [(1 - 0)(1 - 0)] = 0$

Level 1 (OR gate): $Top = 1 - \left[\left(1 - \dfrac{1}{2}\right)(1 - 0) \right] = \dfrac{1}{2}$

where $I_B^{Struc} = \dfrac{7}{8} - \dfrac{1}{2} = \dfrac{3}{8}$

Event C:

(1) Considering $q_C = 1$, $q_i = \dfrac{1}{2} \forall i \neq C$

Level 3 (AND gates): $G_2 = \dfrac{1}{2} \cdot 1 = \dfrac{1}{2}$; $G_3 = \dfrac{1}{2} \cdot \dfrac{1}{2} = \dfrac{1}{4}$

Level 2 (OR gate): $G_1 = 1 - \left[\left(1 - \dfrac{1}{2}\right)\left(1 - \dfrac{1}{4}\right) \right] = \dfrac{5}{8}$

Level 1 (OR gate): $Top = 1 - \left[\left(1 - \dfrac{1}{2}\right)\left(1 - \dfrac{5}{8}\right) \right] = \dfrac{13}{16}$

(2) When $q_C = 0$, $q_i = \dfrac{1}{2} \forall i \neq C$, then

Level 3 (AND gates): $G_2 = \dfrac{1}{2} \cdot 0 = \dfrac{1}{2}$; $G_3 = \dfrac{1}{2} \cdot \dfrac{1}{2} = \dfrac{1}{4}$

Level 2 (OR gate): $G_1 = 1 - \left[(1 - 0)\left(1 - \dfrac{1}{4}\right) \right] = \dfrac{1}{4}$

Level 1 (OR gate): $Top = 1 - \left[\left(1 - \dfrac{1}{2}\right)\left(1 - \dfrac{1}{4}\right) \right] = \dfrac{5}{8}$

being $I_C^{Struc} = \dfrac{13}{16} - \dfrac{5}{8} = \dfrac{3}{16}$

Event D:

Analogously, the importance of this event is: $I_D^{Struc} = \dfrac{13}{16}$.

CASE 3

The Top Event is given by the following logical function:

$$f = A + B(C + DE) = A + BC + BDE$$

The MCSs are:

$$CMS_1 = A$$
$$CMS_2 = BC$$
$$CMS_3 = BDE$$

The probability of occurrence of the Top Event:

$$Q_{sys} = P(A \cup BC \cup BDE)$$
$$= P(A) + P(BC) + P(BDE) - P(A \cap BC) - P(A \cap BDE)$$
$$- P(BC \cap BDE) + P(A \cap BC \cap BDE)$$

$$Q_{sys} = q_A + q_B q_C + q_B q_D q_E - q_A q_B q_C - q_A q_B q_D q_E$$
$$- q_B q_C q_D q_E + q_A q_B q_C q_D q_E$$

For $q_A = q_B = q_C = q_D = q_E = 0.01$, it is obtained that:

$$Q_{sys} = 0.01 + 0.01^2 + 0.01^3 - 0.01^3 - 2(0.01)^4 + 0.01^5 = 0.0101$$

Fussell-Vesely

$$I_A^{FV} = \frac{P(A)}{Q_{sys}} = \frac{q_A}{Q_{sys}} = \frac{0.01}{0.0101} = 0.99$$

$$I_B^{FV} = \frac{P(BC \cup BDE)}{Q_{sys}} = \frac{P(BC) + P(BDE) - P(BC \cap BDE)}{Q_{sys}}$$

$$= \frac{q_B q_C + q_B q_D q_E - q_B q_C q_D q_E}{Q_{sys}} = \frac{0.01^2 - 0.01^3 - 0.01^4}{0.0101} = 0.0099$$

$$I_C^{FV} = \frac{P(BC)}{Q_{sys}} = \frac{q_B q_C}{Q_{sys}} = \frac{0.01^2}{0.0101} = 0.00990$$

$$I_D^{FV} = \frac{P(BCE)}{Q_{sys}} = \frac{q_B q_D q_E}{Q_{sys}} = \frac{0.01^3}{0.0101} = 0.000099$$

Birnbaum

It is necessary to calculate the derivative with respect to each event to obtain the Birnbaum IM:

$$Q_{sys} = q_A + q_B q_C + q_B q_D q_E - q_A q_B q_C - q_A q_B q_D q_E$$
$$- q_B q_C q_D q_E + q_A q_B q_C q_D q_E$$

Thus:

$$I_A^{Birm} = \frac{\partial Q_{sys}}{\partial q_A} = 1 - q_B q_C - q_B q_D q_E + q_B q_C q_D q_E = 1 - 0.01^2 - 0.01^3 + 0.01^4$$
$$= 0.9998$$

$$I_B^{Birm} = \frac{\partial Q_{sys}}{\partial q_B} = q_C - q_D q_E - q_A q_C - q_A q_D q_E - q_C q_D q_E - q_A q_C q_D q_E$$
$$= 1 - 2(0.01)^3 + 0.01^4 = 0.0099$$

$$I_C^{Birm} = \frac{\partial Q_{sys}}{\partial q_C} = q_B - q_A q_B - q_B q_D q_E + q_A q_B q_D q_E$$
$$= 0.01 - 0.01^2 - 0.01^3 + 0.01^4 = 0.0098$$

$$I_D^{Birm} = \frac{\partial Q_{sys}}{\partial q_D} = q_B q_E - q_A q_B q_E - q_B q_C q_E + q_A q_B q_C q_E$$
$$= 0.01^2 - 2(0.01)^3 + 0.01^4 = 0.000098$$

$$I_E^{\text{Birm}} = \frac{\partial Q_{\text{sys}}}{\partial q_{EE}} = q_B q_D q - q_A q_B q_{DE} - q_B q_C q_D + q_A q_B q_C q_D$$

$$= 0.01^2 - 2(0.01)^3 + 0.01^4 = 0.000098$$

AND Criterion

For each event, the number of AND gates are counted from the event to the Top.

Rank	Events	AND gates
1.	A	0
2.	B	1
2.	C	1
3.	D	2
3.	E	2

Heuristic Structural Criterion

The variable ranking given by the TDLR method is: A, B, C, D, and E.

Event A:

(1) Taking $q_A = 1$, $q_i = \frac{1}{2} \forall i \neq A$

Level 4 (AND gate): $G_3 = \frac{1}{2} \cdot \frac{1}{2} = \frac{1}{4}$

Level 3 (OR gate): $G_2 = 1 - \left[\left(1 - \frac{1}{2}\right)\left(1 - \frac{1}{4}\right)\right] = 5/8$

Level 2 (AND gate): $G_1 = \frac{1}{2} \cdot \frac{5}{8} = \frac{5}{16}$

Level 1 (OR gate): $Top = 1 - \left[(1 - 1)\left(1 - \frac{5}{16}\right)\right] = 1$

(2) Considering $q_A = 0$, $q_i = \frac{1}{2} \forall i \neq A$

Level 4 (AND gate): $G_3 = \frac{1}{2} \cdot \frac{1}{2} = \frac{1}{4}$

Level 3 (OR gate): $G_2 = 1 - \left[\left(1 - \frac{1}{4}\right)\left(1 - \frac{1}{4}\right)\right] = 7/16$

Level 2 (AND gate): $G_1 = \frac{1}{2} \cdot \frac{5}{8} = \frac{5}{16}$

Level 1 (OR gate): $Top = 1 - \left[(1 - 0)\left(1 - \frac{5}{16}\right)\right] = \frac{5}{16}$

Being $I_A^{\text{Struc}} = 1 - \frac{5}{16} = 11/16$

Event *B*:

(1) Taking $q_B = 1$, $q_i = \frac{1}{2} \forall i \neq B$

Level 4 (AND gate): $G_3 = \frac{1}{2} \cdot \frac{1}{2} = \frac{1}{4}$

Level 3 (OR gate): $G_2 = 1 - \left[\left(1 - \frac{1}{2}\right)\left(1 - \frac{1}{4}\right)\right] = \frac{5}{8}$

Level 2 (AND gate): $G_1 = 1 \cdot \frac{5}{8} = \frac{5}{8}$

Level 1 (OR gate): $Top = 1 - \left[\left(1 - \frac{1}{2}\right)\left(1 - \frac{5}{8}\right)\right] = \frac{13}{16}$

(2) When $q_B = 0$, $q_i = \frac{1}{2} \forall i \neq B$, then

Level 4 (AND gate): $G_3 = \frac{1}{2} \cdot \frac{1}{2} = \frac{1}{4}$

Level 3 (OR gate): $G_2 = 1 - \left[\left(1 - \frac{1}{2}\right)\left(1 - \frac{1}{4}\right)\right] = \frac{5}{8}$

Level 2 (AND gate): $G_1 = 0 \cdot \frac{5}{8} = 0$

Level 1 (OR gate): $Top = 1 - \left[\left(1 - \frac{1}{2}\right)(1 - 0)\right] = \frac{1}{2}$

Being $I_B^{Struc} = \frac{13}{16} - \frac{1}{2} = \frac{5}{16}$

Event *C*:

(1) Considering $q_C = 1$, $q_i = \frac{1}{2} \forall i \neq C$

Level 4 (AND gate): $G_3 = \frac{1}{2} \cdot \frac{1}{2} = \frac{1}{4}$

Level 3 (OR gate): $G_2 = 1 - \left[(1 - 1)\left(1 - \frac{1}{4}\right)\right] = 1$

Level 2 (AND gate): $G_1 = \frac{1}{2} \cdot 1 = \frac{1}{2}$

Level 1 (OR gate): $Top = 1 - \left[\left(1 - \frac{1}{2}\right)\left(1 - \frac{1}{2}\right)\right] = \frac{3}{4}$

(2) Taking into account $q_C = 0$, $q_i = \frac{1}{2} \forall i \neq C$

Level 4 (AND gate): $G_3 = \frac{1}{2} \cdot \frac{1}{2} = \frac{1}{4}$

Level 3 (OR gate): $G_2 = 1 - \left[(1 - 0)\left(1 - \frac{1}{4}\right)\right] = \frac{1}{4}$

Level 2 (AND gate): $G_1 = \frac{1}{2} \cdot \frac{1}{4} = \frac{1}{8}$

Level 1 (OR gate): $Top = 1 - \left[\left(1 - \frac{1}{2} \right) \left(1 - \frac{1}{8} \right) \right] = \frac{9}{16}$

Therefore $I_C^{\text{Struc}} = \frac{3}{4} - \frac{9}{16} = \frac{3}{16}$

Event D:

(1) Considering $q_D = 1$, $q_i = \frac{1}{2} \forall i \neq D$

Level 4 (AND gate): $G_3 = 1 \cdot \frac{1}{2} = \frac{1}{2}$

Level 3 (OR gate): $G_2 = 1 - \left[\left(1 - \frac{1}{2} \right) \left(1 - \frac{1}{2} \right) \right] = \frac{3}{4}$

Level 2 (AND gate): $G_1 = \frac{1}{2} \cdot \frac{3}{4} = \frac{3}{8}$

Level 1 (OR gate): $Top = 1 - \left[\left(1 - \frac{1}{2} \right) \left(1 - \frac{3}{8} \right) \right] = \frac{11}{16}$

(2) Taking into account $q_D = 0$, $q_i = \frac{1}{2} \forall i \neq D$

Level 4 (AND gate): $G_3 = 0 \cdot \frac{1}{2} = 0$

Level 3 (OR gate): $G_2 = 1 - \left[\left(1 - \frac{1}{2} \right) (1 - 0) \right] = \frac{1}{2}$

Level 2 (AND gate): $G_1 = \frac{1}{2} \cdot \frac{1}{2} = \frac{1}{4}$

Level 1 (OR gate): $Top = 1 - \left[\left(1 - \frac{1}{2} \right) \left(1 - \frac{1}{4} \right) \right] = \frac{5}{8}$

Therefore $I_D^{\text{Struc}} = \frac{11}{16} - \frac{5}{8} = 1/16$

Event E:

This case is the same as that of event D (it is under the same gate):

$$I_E^{\text{Struc}} = \frac{1}{16}$$

In summary, the following tables allow a comparison of the different methods used to generate the rankings of events in each LDT.

Table D.1 shows that the same rankings are obtained for every method. A simple example has been chosen to illustrate clearly that in some cases it is possible to get the same results. The LDT in Fig. D.2 is very simple and no calculations are required. In this case, the AND criterion reduces the computational cost and provides the same results. The ranking of events at the

Table D.1 Rankings considering the different methods for the example 1

Basic events	Fussell-Vesley I_i^{FV} (rank)	Birnbaum I_i^{Birn} (rank)	AND criterion N° gates (rank)	Heuristic structural criterion I_i^{Struc} (rank)
A	0.980584 (1)	0.9998 (1)	0 (1)	$\dfrac{9}{16}$ (1)
B	0.009806 (2)	0.0099 (2)	1 (2)	$\dfrac{3}{16}$ (2)
C	0.009806 (2)	0.0099 (2)	1 (2)	$\dfrac{3}{16}$ (2)
D	0.009806 (2)	0.0099 (2)	1 (2)	$\dfrac{3}{16}$ (2)
E	0.009806 (2)	0.0099 (2)	1 (2)	$\dfrac{3}{16}$ (2)

same level is performed randomly. Any of the 16 possible rankings is valid (permutations of 4 elements, $4! = 16$).

Table D.2 shows the results of the example given in Fig. D.2. This is a modification of the LDT in Example 1, where some events have been replaced. Table D.2 shows that Fussell-Vesely, Birnbaum, and heuristic criterion provide the same ranking, the last method being the most efficient because it needs a lower computational cost. In this case, the AND criterion is not sufficient to obtain a good ranking because it places the event B at the same level than events C and D, and it should appear above them, because it is a MOE and, therefore, it has more influence in the LDT.

Table D.2 Resulting rankings according to the different methods for example 2

Basic events	Fussell-Vesley I_i^{FV} (rank)	Birnbaum I_i^{Birn} (rank)	AND criterion N° gates (rank)	Heuriustic structural criterion I_i^{Heur} (rank)
A	0.980681 (1)	0.9998 (1)	0 (1)	$\dfrac{9}{16}$ (1)
B	0.019516 (2)	0.0197 (2)	1 (2)	$\dfrac{3}{8}$ (2)
C	0.009807 (3)	0.0098 (3)	1 (2)	$\dfrac{3}{16}$ (3)
D	0.009807 (3)	0.0098 (3)	1 (2)	$\dfrac{3}{16}$ (3)

Table D.3 Resulting rankings according to the different methods for example 3

Basic events	Fussell-Vesely I_i^{FV} (rank)	Birnbaum I_i^{Birn} (rank)	AND criterion N° gates (rank)	Heuriustic structural criterion I_i^{Heur} (rank)
A	0.990099 (1)	0.999899 (1)	0 (1)	$\frac{11}{16}$ (1)
B	0.00999 (2)	0.009998 (2)	1 (2)	$\frac{5}{16}$ (2)
C	0.00989 (3)	0.009899 (3)	1 (2)	$\frac{3}{16}$ (3)
D	0.00009 (4)	0.000098 (4)	2 (3)	$\frac{1}{16}$ (4)
E	0.00009 (4)	0.000098 (4)	2 (3)	$\frac{1}{16}$ (4)

Table D.3 provides similar conclusions. It can be observed that the same ranking is provided by Fussell Vesely, Birnbaum, and the proposed heuristic. The AND criterion differs from the other methods because it places events B and C at the same level of importance, although they are in different levels of the LDT.

REFERENCES

1. Bywater, I. *Aristotelis Ethica Nicomachea.* Parker, 1880.
2. Briner, B. *The Management Methods of Jesus: Ancient Wisdom for Modern Business.* Thomas Nelson Incorporated, 1996.
3. Fitzgerald, S. P. *Decision Making.* Capstone Pub., 2002.
4. Piffano, H. L. P. El dilema de condorcet-el problema de la votación por mayoría simple de duncan black-la paradoja de kenneth arrow-y el manejo de agenda. *Documentos de Trabajo* **2009**.
5. Klein, H. K.; Hirschheim, R. Fundamental Issues of Decision Support Systems: A Consequentialist Perspective. *Decis. Support. Syst.* **1985**, *1*, 5–23.
6. Burstein, F.; Holsapple, C. *Handbook on Decision Support Systems 2: Variations.* Springer Science & Business Media, 2008.
7. Kanigel, R. *The One Best Way: Frederick Winslow Taylor and the Enigma of Efficiency (Sloan Technology).* The MIT Press, 2005.
8. Gigerenzer, G.; Selten, R. *Bounded Rationality: The Adaptive Toolbox.* MIT Press, 2002.
9. Novicevic, M. M.; Clayton, R. W.; Williams, W. A. Barnard's Model of Decision Making: A Historical Predecessor of Image Theory. *J. Manage. Hist.* **2011**, *17*, 420–434.
10. Wald, A. Statistical Decision Functions. *Ann. Math. Stat.* **1949**, ;165–205.
11. Zadeh, L. A. Fuzzy Sets. *Inform. Control* **1965**, *8*, 338–353.
12. Savage, L. J. *The Foundations of Statistics, New York*, 1954.
13. Von Neumann, J.; Morgenstern, O. *Theory of Games and Economic Behavior.* Princeton University Press, 2007.
14. Gordon, S.; Mulligan, P. Strategic Models for the Delivery of Personal Financial Services: The Role of Infocracy. *Comput. Inform. Technol. Hum. Side* **2003**, 220.
15. Asghar, S. A Survey on Multi-Criteria Decision Making Approaches, Emerging Technologies, ICET 2009. *International Conference on IEEE*, 2009; pp 321–325.
16. Ekárt, A.; Németh, S. Z. Stability Analysis of Tree Structured Decision Functions. *Eur. J. Operat. Res.* **2005**, *160*, 676–695.
17. Baker, D.; Bridges, D.; Hunter, R.; Johnson, G.; Krupa, J.; Murphy, J.; Sorenson, K. *Guidebook to Decision Making Methods.* Department of Energy: USA, 2002.
18. Harris, R. Introduction to Decision Making, Virtualsalt, 1998. http://www.virtualsalt.com/crebook5.htm (accessed 09.10.11).
19. Forrester, J. W. *System Dynamics and the Lessons of 35 Years. A Systems-Based Approach to Policymaking*; Springer, 1993; pp. 199-240.
20. Huber, G. P.; Peters, T.; Waterman, R.; Salinas, A.; Bradford, C.; Moneta, C.; Acevedo Garat, M.; Barkim, D.; Suárez, B.; Villanueva Marrufo, A. *Toma de decisiones en la gerencia.* CIMMYT: México, DF (México), 1984.
21. Villegas-García, M. A.; Márquez, F. P. G.; Tercero, D. J. P. *How Business Analytics Should Work. Advanced Business Analytics*; Springer, 2015; pp. 93-108.
22. Claver Cortés, E.; Llopis Taverner, J.; Lloret Llinares, M.; Molina Manchon, H. *Manual de administración de empresas.* Cívitas: Madrid, 1994.
23. Pliego Marugán, A.; García Márquez, F. P.; Lorente, J. Decision Making Process via Binary Decision Diagram. *Int. J. Manage. Sci. Eng. Manage.* **2015**, *10*, 3–8.
24. Kull, T. J.; Oke, A.; Dooley, K. J. Supplier Selection Behavior Under Uncertainty: Contextual and Cognitive Effects on Risk Perception and Choice. *Decis. Sci.* **2014**, *45*, 467–505.
25. Fülöp, J. In *Introduction to Decision Making Methods*, BDEI-3 Workshop, Washington; Citeseer, 2005.

26. Wan, S.-P.; Wang, F.; Dong, J.-Y. A Novel Group Decision Making Method With Intuitionistic Fuzzy Preference Relations for RFID Technology Selection. *Appl. Soft Comput.* **2016**, *38*, 405–422.

27. Cascetta, E.; Carteni, A.; Pagliara, F.; Montanino, M. A New Look at Planning and Designing Transportation Systems: A Decision-Making Model Based on Cognitive Rationality, Stakeholder Engagement and Quantitative Methods. *Transp. Policy* **2015**, *38*, 27–39.

28. Zhang, Z.; Guo, C. Notes on "Logarithmic Least Squares Method to Priority for Group Decision Making With Incomplete Fuzzy Preference Relations" *Appl. Math. Model.* **2016**, *40*, 1788–1792.

29. Manupati, V.; Anand, R.; Thakkar, J.; Benyoucef, L.; Garsia, F. P.; Tiwari, M. Adaptive Production Control System for a Flexible Manufacturing Cell Using Support Vector Machine-Based Approach. *Int. J. Adv. Manuf. Technol.* **2013**, *67*, 969–981.

30. Wu, A. P.; Chapman, P. L. Simple Expressions for Optimal Current Waveforms for Permanent-Magnet Synchronous Machine Drives. *IEEE Trans. Energy Convers.* **2005**, *20*, 151–157.

31. Wu, D. D.; Olson, D. L., Luo, C. A Decision Support Approach for Accounts Receivable Risk Management. *IEEE Trans. Syst. Man Cybernet. Syst.* **2014**, *44*, 1624–1632.

32. Wu, D.; Olson, D. L.; Dolgui, A. Decision Making in Enterprise Risk Management: A Review and Introduction to Special Issue. *Omega* **2015**, *57*, 1–4.

33. Márquez, F. G.; Papaelias, J. P. P. M.; Hermosa, R. R. Wind Turbines Maintenance Management Based on FTA and BDD. In *International Conference on Renewable Energies and Power Quality (ICREPQ'12)*, 2012; pp 4–6.

34. de la Hermosa González, R. R.; Márquez, F. P. G.; Dimlaye, V.; Ruiz-Hernández, D. Pattern Recognition by Wavelet Transforms Using Macro Fibre Composites Transducers. *Mech. Syst. Signal Process.* **2014**, *48*, 339–350.

35. García Márquez, F. P.; García-Pardo, I. P. Principal Component Analysis Applied to Filtered Signals for Maintenance Management. *Qual. Reliab. Eng. Int.* **2010**, *26*, 523–527.

36. Márquez, F. P. G. A new Method for Maintenance Management Employing Principal Component Analysis. *Struct. Durability Health Monit.* **2010**, *6*, 89–99.

37. Jahan, A.; Edwards, K. L. *Multi-Criteria Decision Analysis for Supporting the Selection of Engineering Materials in Product Design.* Butterworth-Heinemann, 2013.

38. Marquez, F. Binary Decision Diagrams Applied to Fault Tree Analysis [c]. *4th LET International Conference on Railway Condition Monitoring*, 2008; pp 126–128.

39. Márquez, F. P. G.; Pérez, J. M. P.; Marugán, A. P.; Papaelias, M. Identification of Critical Components of Wind Turbines Using FTA Over the Time. *Renew. Energy* **2016**, *87*, 869–883.

40. Pliego Marugán, A.; García Márquez, F. P.; Pinar Pérez, J. M. Optimal Maintenance Management of Offshore Wind Farms. *Energies* **2016**, *9*, 46.

41. Gomez Munoz, C.; De la Hermosa Gonzalez-Carrato, R.; Trapero Arenas, J.; Garcia Marquez, F. A Novel Approach to Fault Detection and Diagnosis on Wind Turbines. *Global NEST J.* **2014**, *16*, 1029–1037.

42. Marquez, F. G.; Singh, V.; Papaelias, M. A Review of Wind Turbine Maintenance Management Procedures. *The Eighth International Conference on Condition Monitoring and Machinery Failure Prevention Technologies*, 2011; pp 1–14.

43. Mallo, C.; Merlo, J. *Control de gestión y control presupuestario.* McGraw-Hill: Madrid, 1995.

44. Campos, E. B.; Roche, I. C.; Herrera, J. J. D. *Economía de la empresa: Análisis de las decisiones empresariales.* ISBN: 8436802071. Editor: Piramide; 2002.

45. Amat, J. M. *El control de gestión: Una perspectiva de dirección./joan m^a.* Ediciones Gestión: Amat., Barcelona, 2000.

46. García Márquez, F. P.; Moreno, H. *Introduccion al analisis de arboles de fallos: Empleo de bdds.* 2012. ISBN10: 3847356763. ISBN-13: 978-3847356769. Eae Editorial Academia Espanola.

47. Hauptmanns, U. Análisis de árboles de fallos. Bellaterra, 1986.
48. Stamatelatos, M.; Dezfuli, H.; Apostolakis, G.; Everline, C.; Guarro, S.; Mathias, D.; Mosleh, A.; Paulos, T.; Riha, D.; Smith, C. Probabilistic Risk Assessment Procedures Guide for NASA Managers And Practitioners, 2nd ed., 2011, NASA/SP-2011-3421.
49. Galván González, B. J. Contribuciones a la evaluación cuantitativa de árboles de fallos, 1999. University of Las Palmas de Gran Canaria. Doctoral dissertation.
50. Fussell, J. How to Hand-Calculate System Reliability and Safety Characteristics. *IEEE Trans. Reliab.* **1975**, *3*, 169–174.
51. Birnbaum, Z. W. *On the Importance of Different Components in a Multicomponent System.* DTIC Document, 1968.
52. Lambert, H. *Measures of Importance of Events and Cut Sets in Fault Trees.* Lawrence Livermore Lab.: California Univ., Livermore (USA), 1974.
53. Xie, M.; Tan, K.; Goh, K.; Huang, X. Optimum Prioritisation and Resource Allocation Based on Fault Tree Analysis. *Int. J. Qual. Reliab. Manage.* **2000**, *17*, 189–199.
54. Rausand, M.; Høyland, A. *System Reliability Theory: Models, Statistical Methods, and Applications, Vol. 396.* John Wiley & Sons, 2004.
55. Vesley, D. W.; Dugan, D. J.; Fragole, J.; Minarik, J., II; Railsback, J. Fault Tree Handbook With Aerospace Applications. In *NASA Office of Safety and Mission Assurance, NASA Headquarters, Washington DC*; 2002 20546.
56. Mosleh, A.; Fleming, K.; Parry, G.; Paula, H.; Worledge, D.; Rasmuson, D. M. *Procedures for Treating Common Cause Failures in Safety and Reliability Studies: Volume 2, Analytic Background and Techniques: Final Report.* Electric Power Research Inst./Pickard, Lowe and Garrick, Inc: Palo Alto, CA (USA)/Newport Beach, CA (USA), 1988.
57. Moret, B. M. Decision Trees and Diagrams. *ACM Comput. Surv. (CSUR)* **1982**, *14*, 593–623.
58. Akers, S. B. Binary Decision Diagrams. *IEEE Trans. Comput.* **1978**, *100*, 509–516.
59. Bryant, R. E. Graph-Based Algorithms for Boolean Function Manipulation. *IEEE Trans. Comput.* **1986**, *100*, 677–691.
60. Marugán, A. P.; Márquez, F. P. G.; Lavirgen, J. L. Decision Making Via Binary Decision Diagrams: A Real Case Study. In *Proceedings of the Eighth International Conference on Management Science and Engineering Management.* Springer, 2014; pp 215–222.
61. Bryant, R. E. Symbolic Boolean Manipulation With Ordered Binary-Decision Diagrams. *ACM Comput. Surv. (CSUR)* **1992**, *24*, 293–318.
62. Sinnamon, R. M.; Andrews, J. New Approaches to Evaluating Fault Trees. *Reliab. Eng. Syst. Safety* **1997**, *58*, 89–96.
63. Zang, X.; Sun, H.; Trivedi, K. S. *A BDD-Based Algorithm for Reliability Graph Analysis.* Department of Electrical Engineering, Duke University, Tech. Rep., 2000.
64. Lloyd, G. Guideline for the Certification of Condition Monitoring Systems for Wind Turbines, Hamburg, Germany, 2007.
65. Bartlett, L.; Andrews, J. Comparison of Two New Approaches to Variable Ordering for Binary Decision Diagrams. *Qual. Reliab. Eng. Int.* **2001**, *17*, 151–158.
66. Minato, S.-i; Ishiura, N.; Yajima, S. Shared Binary Decision Diagram With Attributed Edges for Efficient Boolean Function Manipulation. In *Design Automation Conference, Proceedings of the 27th ACM/IEEE.* IEEE, 1990; pp 52–57.
67. Nikolskaïa, M.; Rauzy, A.; Sherman, D. J. *Almana: A BDD Minimization Tool Integrating Heuristic and Rewriting Methods, Formal Methods in Computer-Aided Design.* Springer, 1998;100–114.
68. Rauzy, A. New Algorithms for Fault Trees Analysis. *Reliab. Eng. Syst. Safety* **1993**, *40*, 203–211.
69. Ericson, C. A.; Ll, C. Fault Tree Analysis. In *System Safety Conference, Orlando, FL.* 1999; pp 1–9.

70. Malik, S.; Wang, A. R.; Brayton, R. K.; Sangiovanni-Vincentelli, A. Logic Verification Using Binary Decision Diagrams in a Logic Synthesis Environment. In *Computer-Aided Design, ICCAD-88. Digest of Technical Papers, IEEE International Conference on IEEE.* 1988; pp 6–9.

71. Bartlett, L. M.; Andrews, J. D. An Ordering Heuristic to Develop the Binary Decision Diagram Based on Structural Importance. *Reliab. Eng. Syst. Safety* **2001**, *72*, 31–38.

72. Garc, F. P.; Pliego, A.; Trapero, J. R. A New Ranking Method Approach for Decision Making in Maintenance Management. In *Proceedings of the Seventh International Conference on Management Science and Engineering Management* Springer, 2014; pp 27–38.

73. Coudert, O.; Madre, J. C. Metaprime: An Interactive Fault-Tree Analyzer. *IEEE Trans. Reliab.* **1994**, *43*, 121–127.

74. Artigao, E. *Análisis de árboles de fallos mediante diagramas de decisión binarios.* PFC Universidad de Castilla La Mancha, 2009.

75. Márquez, F. P. G.; Pedregal, D. J.; Roberts, C. New Methods for the Condition Monitoring of Level Crossings. *Int. J. Syst. Sci.* **2015**, *46*, 878–884.

76. Roberts, C.; Márquez, F.; Tobias, A. A Pragmatic Approach to the Condition Monitoring of Hydraulic Level Crossing Barriers. *Proc. Inst. Mech. Eng. F J. Rail Rapid Transit* **2010**, *224*, 605–610.

77. Marugán, A. P.; Márquez, F. P. G. A Novel Approach to Diagnostic and Prognostic Evaluations Applied to Railways: A Real Case Study. *Proc. Inst. Mech. Eng. F J. Rail Rapid Transit* **2015**, 0954409715596183.

78. Munoz, J. C.; Márquez, F. G.; Papaelias, M. Railroad Inspection Based on ACFM Employing a Non-Uniform b-Spline Approach. *Mech. Syst. Signal Process.* **2013**, *40*, 605–617.

79. Papaelias, M.; Márquez, F. G.; Muñoz, J. C.; Roberts, C. A b-Spline Approach To Alternating Current Field Measurement for Railroad Inspection. *Industrial Engineering and Engineering Management. IEEM 2008. IEEE International Conference on IEEE,* 2008; pp 1385–1389.

80. Muñoz, C. Q. G.; Marquez, F. P. G.; Liang, C.; Maria, K.; Abbas, M.; Mayorkinos, P. A New Condition Monitoring Approach for Maintenance Management in Concentrate Solar Plants. In *Proceedings of the Ninth International Conference on Management Science and Engineering Management.* Springer, 2015; pp 999–1008.

81. Márquez, F. P. G.; Muñoz, J. M. C. A Graphic Computerised Maintenance Management System for Fault Detection, Supervision and Safety of the Railway Infrastructure. *IFAC Proc. Vol.* **2009**, *42*, 1629–1634.

82. Jiménez, A. A.; Muñoz, C. Q. G.; Marquez, F. P. G.; Zhang, L. Artificial Intelligence for Concentrated Solar Plant Maintenance Management. In *Proceedings of the Tenth International Conference on Management Science and Engineering Management* Springer, 2017; pp 125–134.

83. Marugán, A. P.; Márquez, F. P. G.; Papaelias, M. Multivariable Analysis for Advanced Analytics of Wind Turbine Management. In *Proceedings of the Tenth International Conference on Management Science and Engineering Management* Springer, 2017; pp 319–328.

84. Márquez, F. P. G.; Muñoz, J. M. C. A Pattern Recognition and Data Analysis Method for Maintenance Management. *Int. J. Syst. Sci.* **2012**, *43*, 1014–1028.

85. M'arquez, F. P. G. I.; Nieto, M. R. M. I. Recurrent Neural Network and Genetic Algorithm Approaches for a Dual Route Optimization Problem: A Real Case Study. In *Proceedings of the Sixth International Conference on Management Science and Engineering Management* Springer, 2013; pp 23–37.

86. Pedregal, P. *Introduction to Optimization, Vol. 46.* Springer Science & Business Media, 2006.

87. Works, T. M. Matlab the Language of Technical Computing. *MATLAB Funct. Ref.* **2001**, *1*.

INDEX

Note: Page numbers followed by *f* indicate figures, *t* indicate tables, and *b* indicate boxes.

Printed in the United States
By Bookmasters